SAUNTERING TO SANTIAGO

THE CAMINO DE SANTIAGO FOR SLOW WALKERS

KENNETH CLINE

MOT-MOT PUBLISHING

The events related in this account are true, based on the author's experiences walking the Caminho Portugues da Costa in August/September 2018.

ISBN: 978-0-9979415-5-5

Photos: Bina Cline

Cover Photo: Bina Cline

❀ Created with Vellum

In loving gratitude to Bina, my wife and best friend, without whom neither this journey nor this book would have been possible.

"I don't like either the word [hike] or the thing. People ought to saunter in the mountains - not 'hike!' Do you know the origin of that word saunter? It's a beautiful word. Away back in the middle ages, people used to go on pilgrimages to the Holy Land, and when people in the villages through which they passed asked where they were going they would reply, 'A la sainte terre', 'To the Holy Land.' And so they became known as sainte-terre-ers or saunterers. Now these mountains are our Holy Land, and we ought to saunter through them reverently, not 'hike' through them."
— Naturalist John Muir

The Camino is not a hike; it is a chance to dip your toe into the river of life that is always flowing there. – Author Unknown

INTRODUCTION

When my wife and I tell people that we walked the Camino de Santiago — over 200 miles from Porto, Portugal, to Santiago de Compostela in Spain — they often respond, "Oh, we've been thinking about doing that too."

So, why don't you? I mean, just go and do it? Why keep the Camino as a forever-unchecked item on your bucket list?

This question is particularly pertinent to people in my age group, mid-60s and older. Many of them possess the time and money to do the Camino de Santiago, or some part of it. Having retired from their full-time jobs and enjoying some reasonable level of health and financial security, they are looking to fulfill some of those dream projects that have been sitting "on the shelf" all these years. Perhaps inspired by films such as *The Way* with Martin Sheen, or all the articles about spiritual self-renewal on the Camino, they may be thinking: Gee, I'd love to do that, but can I really handle it at my age? Can I do all that walking when I lack the physical fitness I might have had 20 years before?

Yes you can, as I will explain in the chapters that follow. Walking the Camino may seem intimidating at first glance but is absolutely doable for people who are well past their 20s and 30s.

In fact, nearly 20% of the 327,000 people who finished the walk in 2018 were over the age of 60. It's just a matter of planning realistically around your individual limitations.

My wife and I, for example, had good reasons at first for worrying about whether walking 200 miles across Portugal and Spain lay outside our comfort zone. I'm 64, with some arthritis and lower back issues. Bina is a few years younger, but struggles with Type 2 diabetes, asthma and high blood pressure. The diabetes, particularly, complicates life when we travel because she needs to take certain medications every day and avoid carbohydrates in her diet.

Yet, as you will see, we learned to plan around those issues and get on with the journey. We're glad we did because we got to experience one of the most joyous achievements of our lives. You can too, as long as you commit yourself to doing the Camino *at your own chosen speed.*

This way to Santiago de Compostela.

1

WHO'S TURTLING NOW?

It was mid-morning on the Portuguese coast when Bina and I came striding up to three other *peregrinos* (pilgrims). The two middle-aged men and a woman blocked our way on the sidewalk leading from the town of Vila Praia de Âncora. The two decidedly overweight men conversed in a language that sounded to us like Portuguese, languidly poking the air with their trekking poles, as the woman strolled alongside. This wouldn't do.

"*Perdoe-me, por favor,*" (Excuse me, please) I said, as the woman stepped aside to let us pass on the left side. Breezing by with the "*Bom Camino*" (Happy Trails) salute that one *peregrino* customarily gives to another, I noticed that all three wore T-shirts emblazoned with the Brazilian national flag.

A few minutes later, I looked back to see them receding into the distance behind us, exclaiming, "They're just *turtling* along!"

Bina and I shared smiles, glorying in our superior state of fitness. However, not more than 20 minutes later, we became aware of a young couple looming up fast behind us. We sped up a little to stay ahead but they gained ground steadily. Nothing we could do but step aside and watch them lope past with purposeful, easy strides that we could in no way match. So, who's turtling now?

We found a lesson in that. The key for older folks walking the Camino de Santiago is to ignore the pace set by other walkers and do it in a style that's convenient to you. At the end of the day, after all, it's *your* Camino.

Begin with the fact that the Camino is actually comprised of seven major trails, with varying degrees of difficulty, all leading to Santiago de Compostela from different countries and different points on the compass. You can pick the route that fits your level of conditioning. We chose the coastal trail up from Portugal because it featured mostly level ground and nice ocean views.

Once you've selected a route, you can decide how many days you want to take and at what level of comfort. The itineraries plotted out in most guidebooks can be modified to shorten or lengthen distances as you see fit.

Also, a wide array of services has developed on the Camino in recent decades to enable you to progress in a style tailored to your needs. Some companies offer a soup-to-nuts experience, providing all of your lodgings, meals and gear transportation. All you have to do each morning is walk along in a guided group as a van lingers close at hand to provide water, snacks and medical assistance.

At the low-cost end, you can rough it by carrying all your gear on your back and staying in *albergues* (group hostels), which charge just over $10 a night.

Between those extremes, you can pick and choose from an à la carte menu of individual services, such as daily luggage transfer or pre-booking of your accommodations. We opted for luggage transfer, enabling us to walk the trail with lightweight day packs, but booked our own lodgings. For comfort and privacy reasons, we chose hotels rather than *albergues*.

The key principle guiding our strategy was: take your time. We spent 32 days covering the 317 kilometers between Porto and

Santiago de Compostela. This is a journey that most guide books suggest that you accomplish in two weeks. In fact, Bina and I walked only 17 of the 32 days, which left a lot of rest days.

As a general rule, we found that keeping our daily pace to just under 20 km and spending one day off the trail for every two days on worked well for us. We usually regretted those days when we pushed it past 25 km, which just plain wore us out.

Were we embarrassed by our leisurely pace? Not a bit. We enjoyed the scenery along the way and the towns where we idled. We reached the plaza in front of the Santiago cathedral around noon on September 7, 2018, with bodies and feet in good shape — zero blisters! The only significant health issue we encountered during the entire journey was a bout of food poisoning for Bina. Such an episode, which delayed us for two days, could have occurred anywhere.

But the loss of the two days did underscore the importance of maintaining a flexible schedule when doing the Camino. A relatively minor annoyance might have morphed into a major problem had our schedule called for air travel right after reaching Santiago. As it was, we did have to reschedule our accommodations and luggage transfer services for the next week after Bina got sick. We adjusted easily because our plans called for remaining on the Iberian Peninsula for another month.

Not everyone will enjoy the luxury of that much time. But it helps to build buffers into your schedule to accommodate the unexpected.

Conceptually, it had always been our intention to "saunter" to Santiago. That was a word we consciously used, since it conveyed the idea of a leisurely ramble. Let others hike, we'll just s-a-u-n-t-e-r along, thank you very much!

Adopting this concept put us in good company. After we had returned to the States, we came upon the quote at the front of this book by the famous American naturalist John Muir (co-founder of the Sierra Club) explaining why he preferred the word "saunter" over "hike." Muir even traced the origins of the word "saunter" to medieval pilgrimages, which applies directly to the special stature or mystique of the Camino de Santiago itself.

The Camino originated nearly 1,000 years ago to serve a particular purpose: pilgrimage to the reputed burial place of St. James the Apostle in Santiago de Compostela.[1] By the 12th century, Santiago had became one of Christendom's top three pilgrimage sites, after Jerusalem and Rome. Men and women of every social standing, including a queen of Portugal and St. Francis of Assisi, left their homes in Europe to journey by various routes to the cathedral at Santiago, where they would seek penance for their sins by visiting the Apostle's tomb.

This practice of pilgrimage began to wane in the 16th century following the Protestant Reformation and the gradual secularization of European society. By the early 1980s, the pilgrimage office in Santiago was recording only a few hundred visitors a year. Fast forward to 2018, when the number reached 327,378. What made the difference?

A visit to the Santiago Cathedral by Pope John Paul II in 1982 helped, as did the decision by UNESCO the following year to declare Santiago de Compostela a World Heritage site. Then there's the proselytizing work of Father Elías Valiña Sampedro, priest of the Galician village of O Cebreiro.

Having written his doctoral thesis on the history of the Camino, Fr. Sampedro set upon the mission of making the route more recognizable and accessible to modern-day pilgrims. During the 1980s, he enlisted the help of mayors in towns along the way, as well as various private associations, to publicize and better define the route. The latter effort included Sampedro driving his old Citröen around northern Spain to paint yellow arrows on rocks, walls and pavement pointing in the direction of Santiago.

Some Spanish Civil Guards once stopped Fr. Sampedro, yellow paint can in hand, a short distance from the French border and asked his business. His response: "Preparing a great invasion from France."

The priest was only having a little fun with the policemen. Yet, his words became prophetic in that more than half the pilgrims arriving in Santiago each year travel on the *Camino Frances*, or French Way, which originates in the French town of Saint-Jean-Pied-de-Port in the Pyrenees.

As the Camino routes became systematized and better delineated, books and movies helped spread the word. A 2010 film, *The Way,* starring Martin Sheen, contributed enormously, particularly in North America. In 2010, U.S. passport holders comprised only 1.2% of the *peregrinos* reaching Santiago. That percentage had jumped to 5.7 by 2018.

The story relates how a doctor (Sheen) begins hiking the Camino in the footsteps of his son, who had been killed by lightning in the Pyrenees. While *The Way* carefully avoids any religious or Catholic themes per se, the major characters do endeavor to "find" themselves on the Camino by overcoming problems that had burdened them in the past. This kind of non-Catholic spirituality is one aspect separating the modern Camino from the older pilgrimage tradition and may account for the broadening of its appeal.

The pilgrimage concept, however, remains central to the Camino de Santiago experience. People who walk the Camino are still referred to as *peregrinos* (Spanish for "pilgrims"). Signs posted at restaurants along the way invite all these *peregrinos* to try their "Pilgrim's Menu," basically the plate of the day. Upon reaching Santiago, *peregrinos* customarily celebrate their achievement by attending the special Pilgrims Mass in the cathedral, which is held every day at noon.

Finally, in order to receive the official *Compostela*, or church-issued certificate testifying to the completion of the journey, they must stand in line in the Pilgrims Office, located near the cathedral, to show two stamps per day for the last 100 km of the walk.

These stamps, gathered from churches, tourist offices or eating/lodging places along the way, are collected in a kind of passport, the *Credencial del Peregrino* (Pilgrim's Credential), purchased before the journey.

Stamp collecting is an important part of the Camino experience.

At no point along the way does the Catholic Church require or even encourage anyone to adhere to its particular creed. But for informational purposes, it does inquire about your motivations for undertaking the trek when you apply for your *Compostela* at the Pilgrim's Office. As you hand in your *Credencial* for scrutiny — a nervous moment if you missed a stamp! — the volunteer staffer will ask if you were guided by one of three motivations: religious, cultural (touristic, actually) and spiritual, which is a blend of religious and cultural.

These are broad enough categories for anyone to find a place. The 2018 breakdown was 43% religious, 48% spiritual and 9% cultural. One can fairly conclude that some notion of personal quest motivates most modern *peregrinos*, although this could range from finding God to losing weight.

Personal quest certainly applied to Bina and me in 2018, as we were dealing with some major changes in our lives. Both of us had retired by this time, she in 2014 and I two years later. In early 2018, we sold our house in Atlanta and embarked upon a new lifestyle as "senior nomads," or retirees with no fixed base. Such a mode of living promised more freedom and travel opportunities, but also potential pitfalls. Would we miss having a "home" to return to, with its network of friends and social activities?

For us, the long days of sauntering to Santiago de Compostela provided a welcome opportunity to contemplate the future ahead and reflect upon past choices — a bit of soul-searching, if you will.

And, if God decided to whisper some guidance to us along the way, so much the better.

---

1. For more on St. James, see Appendix One.

2

WHICH CAMINO?

Bina deserves the credit for first giving us the idea of walking the Camino. Ann Bone, a former colleague of hers from the commercial real estate business, had done so in the summer of 2016, trekking all the way to Santiago from the French border, a distance of 500 miles. As Bina followed Ann's account on Facebook, she noted that Ann was roughly the same age as us and likely at a similar level of physical fitness.

"You know," she commented to me one evening, "there's no reason why we couldn't do something like that, as long as we both stay healthy."

The idea sat there, in the back of our minds, for another year. Then, in the fall of 2017, we began planning our next trip to Europe. We had travelled there often over the last few decades, spending a couple of weeks at a time, mostly in sunny places such as Provence, Crete, Languedoc, Andalusia and Tuscany. This time, we were thinking of something more ambitious.

The Schengen Zone visa rules allow Americans to stay up to three months in the European Union at one time. Why not take full advantage of that? In the past, we had expressed frustration when we had to terminate our visits just as we had settled into a place and begun to feel comfortable. Now that we were both retired, there was no reason we could not stretch a trip out to the full three months.

The issue then became how to make the most of that longer stay. Three months is a long time to just knock around looking at old churches and museums. What could we do that would be different? Truly memorable? That's when Bina remembered Ann Bone's Facebook postings and suggested we begin taking a serious look at the Camino de Santiago.

The more we considered the idea, the more we liked it. Strolling through Spain from one quaint village to another definitely had romantic appeal. What better way to see a country than by walking through it?

We did have some concerns to overcome, such as our lack of experience with long distance walking. In the early years of our marriage, over 30 years ago, we had done a few overnight backpacking trips on the Appalachian Trail. But since then, we had confined ourselves mostly to casual day walks in state and national parks. Tackling the Camino would require an upgrade in our physical conditioning, as well as a total equipment outfitting.

And then there was Bina's medical situation, particularly the diabetes. Spending weeks walking through rural areas with limited services might tax her ability to maintain a proper blood sugar level. Or, it might not. We just didn't know. So, we needed to do some research and come up with a plan to address these concerns.

Fortunately, Bina and I have a division of labor that works pretty well when it comes to research. I scout around the Web, compiling folders of articles to answer the 30,000-feet questions, such as: Is the Camino doable for people our age? What's the best time of year to go? What are the transportation options?

Bina, our wizard with social media, then delves deeper into the details, the practical dos and don'ts compiled by people with first-hand experience. Over the years, she has discovered that virtually every potential travel spot and activity features a forum or blog devoted to that topic, often on Facebook. Want to spend some time in a specific town in the Portuguese Algarve? You can be sure somebody has commented about that experience somewhere on social media.

That's certainly true of the Camino de Santiago, which attracts over 325,000 walkers *each year*. A huge number of these people leave their stories and advice on social media. You can spend countless hours reading this stuff and just skim the surface.[1]

Bina's strategy is to join some of these forums and Facebook groups and monitor the activity. Over time, this enabled her to get a pretty comprehensive picture of what is involved with walking the Camino on a day-to-day basis. She even found comments from diabetics with helpful tips on how to manage their blood sugar issues. A month or two of this research gave us confidence that we could indeed handle the Camino.

Moving on from there, the next question was: which Camino? At least seven major routes wend their way to Santiago de Compostela from France, Portugal and various places in Spain itself. Each of these paths features its own pros and cons in terms of scenery, weather, accommodations and difficulty of terrain.

Dropping down further in that decision tree, you need to decide whether you want to complete an entire route or simply a section. To receive your *Compostela* (certificate of completion) from the Pilgrims Office in Santiago, you need to prove that you walked at least the last 100 km of your chosen route. So, do you want to do the minimum, or more? What can you realistically accomplish in the time allotted?

The most popular route, by far, is the *Camino Frances*, which originates in the Pyrenees, on the French side of the border, and traverses the northern part of Spain's *meseta central* (interior plateau). More than half of all *peregrinos* take the French route, which is the most developed in terms of accommodations and eating places.

The second most walked is the route from Portugal, with most *peregrinos* starting from Porto.[2] Three of the other five, the *Norte* (northern), *Ingles* (English) and *Primitivo* (original), reach Santiago from various places in northern Spain. The *Plata* (silver) starts from Seville, down in the south, and the *Madrid* from Spain's capital.

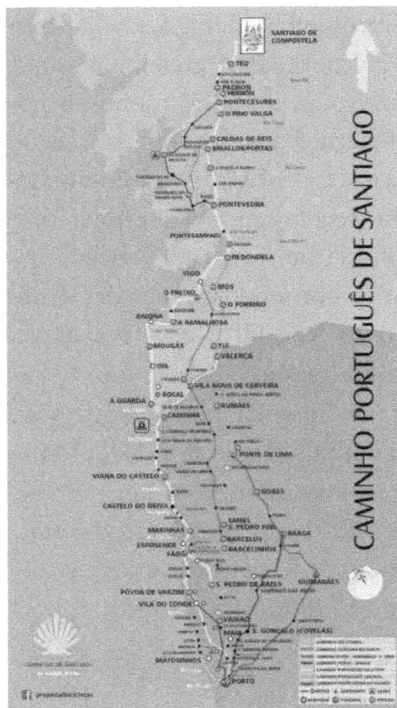

Lots of ways from Porto to Santiago de Compostela.

When Bina and I surveyed these options at the beginning of 2018, the *Caminho Portugues* caught our attention immediately. It would enable us to visit Portugal, a country we had never visited before. And it appeared to have a lower level of technical difficulty, with modest elevations compared to the routes crossing the northern Spanish mountains. Lodging and other infrastructure is also abundant, since tourism is well developed in northern Portugal. Finally, despite its increasing popularity, the *Portugues* doesn't suffer from the over-crowding that afflicts the *Frances*.

Okay, so would be the Portuguese route, but which variation? Technically, the *Portugues* starts in Lisbon, for a total of 600 km to Santiago. Most *peregrinos*, however, commence their walk further north in the coastal city of Porto, which reduces the distance by half. Beyond the problem of length, the Lisbon-to-Porto stretch crosses some thinly populated areas where *albergues* are scarce and lots of time is spent dodging traffic on paved roads, rather than trails.[3] Northern Portugal, by contrast, is chock full of historic cities and towns linked by well-maintained trails.

From Porto, however, you face a choice of two routes north. One trail, known as the "Central," strikes inland from Porto, crossing the Spanish border at Valença do Minho and continuing on to Santiago. The "coastal" variation, as the name implies, parallels the Portuguese coast, crosses into Spain at Caminha and continues on to the Spanish port city of Vigo, where it veers inland to connect with the Central route at Redondela.

To make matters even more complicated, the coastal variation includes its own sub-route, the *Senda Litoral*, which hugs the beaches more. Bina and I mostly utilized the *Senda Litoral* to enjoy the beaches and Atlantic breezes.

The Coastal route for us.

When, then, should we go? Portugal features a mild, sunny climate most of the year so spring, summer and fall were all possible. Rain avoidance governed our decision here. We did not fancy having our walks interrupted by downpours, potentially throwing us off schedule. Nor were we eager to spend our evenings drying out muddy shoes and clothes. Rain just meant trouble, fuss and discomfort all around.

By this measure, summer held the clear advantage, based on very low monthly rain averages in northern Portugal and Spain during that season. But we also knew that beaches in both countries would be inundated with tourists, particularly in August, so we'd be fighting the crowds.

We ended up starting our Camino in the first week of August and finished in the first week of September, which worked out pretty well for us. We did not encounter a single day of rain all the way to Santiago, only a few mornings of mist and fog. And no price could be attached to the joy of walking along a coastal boardwalk on a sunny afternoon to the sound of waves crashing on the rocks, the dunes carpeted in purple heather and the Atlantic breeze cooling your face.

The August tourist hordes did prove a nuisance, at times, by filling up hotel rooms and crowding restaurants. Yet, starting a month or two earlier would have been a disaster, from our point of view, since the region that year experienced one of its wettest springs in recent decades.

---

1. The go-to site right now is the Camino de Santiago Forum hosted by Ivar Rekve. On Facebook, you can look at groups such as American Pilgrims on the Camino, as well as individual groups for each Camino route. Bina found Caminho Portuguese Pilgrims to be particularly helpful.
2. The popularity of the Camino Portugues is rising fast, reaching 20.7% of *Compostelas* issued in 2018, up from 6.4% in 2006.
3. In his book *Portuguese Camino: In Search of the Infinite Moment,* author Terence Callery describes the difficulties of terrain and distance he faced after leaving Lisbon and adds, "On this first day, I was already finding out why so many pilgrims start their Portuguese Camino in Porto."

3

HIGH SCHOOL FIELD TRIP?

Once we had identified our Camino route and best time for undertaking the walk, we faced a more complicated decision: how independent should we be? Or, more precisely, how much support were we going to need along the way?

In past decades, this would not have required any thought because options were very limited. You simply hoisted your backpack and set off for your intended destination, hoping that you found a place to rest your head before nightfall. Grizzled veterans populating the blogs still remember those days fondly — when a *peregrino* was a real pilgrim, almost in the medieval sense, and the open road stretching before you held a lot of uncertainty.

Thanks to the smart phone, today's pilgrims can utilize a GPS-based app to plot their way — a paper map, what's that? These apps also inform you of any cafes and restaurants along the route and your exact distance from them. Google Maps will tell you the days and hours those eating places are open while TripAdvisor rates the quality of the food and service. And room reservations are a cinch with booking.com or hotels.com.

Bina and I got some amusement watching other walkers navigating their way through towns. Although some still look for the yellow arrows and blue and yellow scallop shell signs in the traditional manner, others will keep their eyes glued to their smart phones, like Boy Scouts following a compass.[1]

That's just the way the world has evolved. One wouldn't be going out on too long a limb to state that it's almost impossible to get lost on the Camino nowadays. At least, you'd really have to work at it. Just by possessing a smart phone, the modern *peregrino* possesses a degree of support and convenience unthinkable a few decades ago.

But there's more. An array of services has developed along the Camino routes that enables you to make this walk as easy as you want it to be. Don't want to bother figuring out your route or booking your own lodgings every night? You can hire a company to do that for you. Don't want to carry all your gear on your back each day? Luggage transportation companies can take care of that chore.

Want to feel totally safe and turn your Camino into a real walk in the park? Several companies will do everything for you: pick the route, arrange for all transportation and meals, transport your luggage and have a van hover nearby to provide refreshments and blister repair. In medieval times, even kings didn't travel so well.

All of this pampering comes at a cost, of course, and not just financial. Rebekah Scott, a former travel journalist who is now involved in various Camino-related activities, issued a *cri de coeur* at a conference in Atlanta in 2017 that still attracts a lot of attention on Camino blogs.

Like many Camino veterans, Scott worried that all the modern conveniences are ruining the traditional *peregrino* experience: "On the Camino Frances alone, there are now more than 400 places for pilgrims to spend a night. There are 1,200 places to stop and eat. I am not a statistician, but I can blithely say the number of pilgrim-targeted businesses on the Camino

Frances has quadrupled in the ten years I have lived on the trail.

"The increasing number of pilgrims has attracted the attention of the marketers, the entrepreneurs, the Capitalists. And hereby hangs a conflict."

This conflict, in Scott's view, is between the modern "Consumerist" culture and the "primal simplicity" of the old Camino.

"We want an adventure, but we don't like surprises," she told the conference attendees. "We want all the enlightenment and excitement of a tough hike across a new land, but we want it safe, hygienic, and predictable, served with a smile at less than 20 Euros. We want to stay at the *albergue* everyone else rated best, take the best photos of the local food and wine, write the blog everyone will read.

"And dammit, we want to look pretty and put-together at the end of the day!"

Guilty as charged. Bina and I did all we could to respect the Camino traditions of pilgrimage. And we genuinely admire the people who uphold those traditions.

But, at the same time, maintaining our health on the trail — and yes, comfort — was a priority for us. I had done some rough traveling in my younger days, living in Middle Eastern villages, for example, and no longer have the taste for it. And Bina, with her vulnerable immune system, needs to take special care to avoid getting sick or injured. We made the decision early on that carrying all our gear on our backs and sleeping in hostel bunkbeds every night with 50 people who might snore or spread germs was not an option for us.

Walking the walk was challenge enough. When we rested from our labors at the end of the day, we wanted to relax in a comfortable hotel room and enjoy some of the finer aspects of Portuguese and Spanish cuisine. We make no apologies for wanting to minimize the downsides.

Yet, in retrospect, we made mistakes in our initial planning.

As insecure newbies to the Camino experience, we erred on the side of caution when it came to determining the level of support services that we would need. This story is worth relating for the lessons it might provide to readers weighing their own options.

We started out by looking at companies that offered broad support services. After reading reviews on TripAdvisor and other sites, we focused on two: Marly Camino, based in Madrid, and Follow the Camino, out of Dublin. Each of them provided both guided and self-guided tours, with pre-arranged accommodations and luggage transfer.

Probing a bit deeper, we could see that Marly specialized in the more deluxe guided tours and Follow the Camino in the self-guided. We considered both options, finally settling on Marly. Follow the Camino had trouble designing a self-guided itinerary that seemed leisurely enough for our tastes (not enough sauntering!).

Marly appeared the "safest" option given that they offered full support, meaning people on site, should anything go wrong. Lodgings, meals, itinerary, luggage transfer — Marly had it all covered. All we had to do was get up in the morning and walk with the group.

On the other hand, Bina and I have always been independent travelers. We avoid group tours. The idea of doing our Camino talking to the same group of fellow tourists every day did not appeal. Likewise, Marly's practice of providing its charges with free yellow T-shirts and white day packs emblazoned with the company logo put us off. Good branding for them, but what mature adult wants to relive their high school field trips?

And then there's the cost. You pay through the nose for the soup-to-nuts option. Eleven days on the Portuguese Camino with Marly would cost us an eye-popping $6,800. Obviously, we could do it much cheaper on our own.

However, at this stage in our planning, we were thinking: this is probably a once-in-a-lifetime opportunity, so let's do it right.

Also, time was pressing. By early March, the Marly slots for the Portuguese Camino were rapidly filling up. We felt we had to make a decision, to make some sort of commitment, or this trip would never happen. So, we put down a deposit for a Marly trip that began September 2 and reached Santiago on the 13th.

This deposit came with an escape hatch, however. If we canceled within 60 days of the start of the tour, and before the balance was due, we would forfeit 200 euros ($230). Painful, yes, but not catastrophic. I carefully marked the June 28 deadline on the calendar.

We kept revisiting the issue as the weeks wore on. The more time Bina spent in Camino-related social media, reading the accounts of people actually on the ground, the more she realized that designing our own itinerary and booking our own lodgings was perfectly doable. The one service we definitely needed was luggage transfer, which we could arrange independently.

Luggage transfer was important to us because the Camino constituted only a third of the three-month trip we planned for Portugal and Spain. We would need to take more than hiking clothes and gear to accommodate our subsequent excursions to Barcelona and the Portuguese Algarve. That meant, in addition to day packs needed for the Camino, we had to schlep around with two full roller bags. We needed a service that picked up those bags in the morning and deposited them at the next night's lodging.

Bina's research came up with Tuitrans and Caminofacil as highly recommended companies that covered our chosen route on the Portuguese Camino. Either one would be a whole lot cheaper than Marly.

We debated back and forth as the June 28 date for canceling Marly approached. By May, we had purchased our airline tickets, which had us flying from Atlanta to Lisbon on July 25, returning on October 18. So, we were now committed to the trip one way or another. Canceling Marly at this point would mean re-planning our Camino from scratch and rearranging other items on our itinerary, a lot of hassle to deal with. On the other hand, going with the guided tour never felt right to us. Did it really make any sense to spend all that money when we might do things better and enjoy more flexibility on our own?

The issue wasn't strictly about safety vs. cost. It also had to do with what kind of Camino we wanted to experience. Independent travel felt a bit more "authentic" than a guided tour. As Bina commented one evening, "I want us to experience the Camino in a manner that would be more memorable for us — and more valuable, spiritually." That probably did not include crossing Spain with a gaggle of folks in yellow T-shirts.

In early June we made our decision: cancel Marly and do it ourselves.[2]

---

1. Why scallops? See Appendix Two.
2. During the walk from Porto to Santiago, I was on the lookout for Marly groups but never saw one. However, some friends of ours, John and Caryl Buford, did walk part of the Camino Frances that fall and encountered a yellow-shirted Marly group while having breakfast in a hotel. John said the Marly group received the full attention of the waiters and kitchen staff as he and Caryl sat there, neglected and hungry. Large tour groups like Marly enjoy a lot of clout with vendors on the Camino.

4

PACKING OUR FEARS

D eveloping our own Camino itinerary did prove time-consuming. It's always much harder to plan a trip yourself, which is why some people still hire travel agents. On the other hand, social media and computerized technology make that job a lot easier than it used to be.

In her perusal of the various Facebook groups, Bina had come up with sample itineraries and recommendations on lodging for the Portuguese Camino. This enabled us to broadly map out the major stages of the coastal variation from Porto to Santiago. We then acquired more detailed information from an app called *Wisely Pilgrim*, which we downloaded onto the iPhones and iPads that we would be carrying on the trip.

The beauty of *Wisely Pilgrim* is that it enabled us to track our entire walk via GPS. If we deviated from the official trail, *Wisely* would soon reveal the mistake and show us how to navigate back. The version of this app that covers the Portuguese Camino highlights the route variations, with the interior way to Tui shown in green and the coastal route to Caminha in blue.

Drill down deeper on the coastal path and further variations appear in red, such as the *Senda Litoral* (shore path), which really hugs the beach. *Wisely Pilgrim* also picked up most of the restaurants, *albergues* and hotels we passed along the way. We always had a good idea how far we were from the next rest stop.

As a backup, we installed another app, maps.me, upon which we overlaid a file called *Flannery's Map of Portuguese Camino*. *Flannery* offers more detailed maps than *Wisely*. So, we often found it helpful to compare the two, using *Flannery* when it seemed to offer a better route choice than *Wisely*, or vice versa.

A key benefit of *Wisely* is that it shows the distance between towns in kilometers. Taking some of the sample itineraries that Bina had found on social media, we were able to correlate those with *Wisely* to identify our stopping places for each day of the walk from Porto to Santiago. We also consulted gronze.com, a Spanish language Website that contains detailed maps of all of the various Camino routes, with distance calculations.

Between *Wisely* and *Gronze*, we compiled a spreadsheet plotting out the stages of our Camino and the distances between those stages in both kilometers and miles, along with lodging bookings at each point. Included were notes on special issues involved with some stages, such as a link to the ferry schedule for crossing the Miño River from Portugal into Spain. This remained our basic planning document for the entire trip.

Once we had identified the appropriate stages of our journey, we used booking.com to make our hotel reservations. While there are other hotel booking sites, we found booking.com to be efficient and convenient for our purposes. You pick the day you plan to be in town, see what's available and then check the prices, ratings and reviews, often correlating the latter with those on TripAdvisor.

We particularly liked the fact that booking.com typically offers the opportunity to make refundable reservations, which came in handy several times during the trip. Before we left for Portugal at the end of July, we had our entire Camino planned

and mapped out, from beginning to end, including accommodations.

Yet, as the military knows well, no plan survives the actual
battle. We hadn't spent many days on the trail before we realized
that some of the assumptions in our spreadsheet were overly
optimistic. Those days when we walked much beyond 20 km did
not go well, leaving us tired and over-heated. So, we had to sit
down and revise large parts of the schedule to allow for shorter
distances between stages.

It was at that point that we came up with our two-days-
on/one-day-off formula. After two walking days, we would take
one day off to rest up, do some sightseeing and take care of
laundry and other errands. That formula served us well during
the remaining days to Santiago.

Another big part of our planning process involved buying the
right equipment before we left for Portugal. The month we spent
in Atlanta prior to our departure involved lengthy visits to an REI
store located near the Perimeter Mall. As the saying goes —
which Bina likes repeating — "You pack your fears." This being
our first Camino, we had a few. We could imagine lots of things
going wrong and tried to prepare for every dire possibility.

Nothing impacts a Camino more than accidents or medical
problems and those often involve feet.[1] Blister prevention and
repair is an evergreen topic in Camino blogs and those discus-
sions typically start with the first line of defense: shoes and
socks.[2]

Unfortunately, there's probably too much information available on this topic. The diversity of opinion will make your head
spin. And the reason for that is simple: there is no single shoes-
and-socks combination that works best for everyone. Feet are
stubbornly individual, of different sizes, configurations and stress
resistance. Some people do the Camino in heavy hiking boots,
others in sandals, with most picking some option in between.

The best contribution that I can make is to relate how Bina and I made our decisions and how that worked out for us.

The general consensus nowadays is that heavy hiking boots are out — at least for North Americans. We did notice some Europeans still clumping around along the coast in boots that would have worked in the Alps. In any case, for us the selection narrowed down to either hiking *shoes* (less weight and lower profile than boots) or trail runners (a kind of super-strong athletic shoe).

Hiking shoes, with their thicker treads and stronger ankle support, give you more stability on rough terrain, such as cobblestones or rocks. But, they are also heavier. And those with waterproofing don't "breathe" as well as trail runners, so your feet might sweat more. Trail runners are lighter and more flexible, which improves comfort and ventilation. Their downside is that they don't give you as much support on rough ground.

A lot of your choice should be guided by the Camino route you will be walking. Going to spend a lot of time in the mountains? You might want to opt for hiking shoes. On flatter ground, trail runners should work fine. Our research on the Portuguese route indicated that we would encounter a mixture of coastal boardwalk, some sandy stretches and woods, and plenty of cobblestone streets. So, generally flat, not too much elevation, but occasional rough ground.

Considering that scenario, you could make an argument for both hiking shoes and trail runners. The determining factor then becomes: what feels most comfortable to you, personally?

Bina and I split on this point, with her opting for a trail runner (Hoka One One Stinson ATR 4) and me for a hiking shoe (Keen Targhee III). My Keens just felt right on the day I tested them out in the store. They featured enough room in the tip for my toes to spread out comfortably, but were tight enough in back to prevent slipping in the heel — roomy but snug.

The Keens were also waterproof, which I initially thought

would be helpful. The REI salesman insisted that the mesh around the lacings would enable them to breathe sufficiently. Bina, likewise, couldn't beat the comfort and fit of her Hoka One One trail runner and never looked back.

Not me. This is a good example of where too much research can drive you crazy. The more I read up on the hiking shoe vs. trail runner controversy, the more I questioned my choice. In the forums, many experienced *peregrinos* complained about the heaviness of hiking shoes and asserted that trail runners offered perfectly adequate stability on most any ground.

And that waterproofing on the Keens? More hindrance than help, it seems, because waterproofing on a shoe is never 100% effective. When the leather gets wet, as it will in any serious deluge, the shoe will simply take longer to dry out.

And one more thing. The general rule of thumb is that you should buy a hiking shoe one half to one full size larger than your normal shoe size because feet have a tendency to swell with prolonged walking. I had only gone up half a size in the Keens. Was that enough?

On subsequent visits to REI and other equipment stores, up until the last few days before we left, I would find myself diligently trying on trail runners a size up from my typical 9 regular. None of them felt right and I ended up taking the Keens to Portugal by default, still unsure I had made the right decision.

Not to worry. Neither Bina nor myself sustained a single blister or other foot-related problem on the Camino. Bina loved the comfort and lightness of her Hoka One Ones, which featured a wide enough sole platform to give her sufficient stability on the ground we encountered.

I did marginally better on the cobblestone roads and rocks of the few hills we climbed, yet never felt the shoes were weighing me down. The waterproofing on the Keens remained a question mark because we didn't encounter any rain.

Once you've selected your shoes, other decisions await. Bina and I both substituted orthopedic inserts for the generic ones that came with our shoes. As a diabetic, Bina's feet are sensitive and need additional cushioning. During our practice walks in Atlanta, she noticed that the bottoms of her feet would get sore after a few kilometers. The inserts solved that problem.

For me, the issue was "over-pronation," which means that that I walk on the inside of my soles. This makes my shoes wear out faster than normal as the tread shears off on the inside. Inserts compensate for that pronation effect.

Avoiding blisters requires some consideration of sock and liner options. Socks need to be strong enough to protect you from shoe friction but must "breathe" enough to avoid moisture buildup, particularly in the toes. Liners provide insulation from the socks and enhance the diffusion of moisture. There are sock brands that claim to provide sufficient insulation and breathability so that liners are not required.[3] Bina and I, however, opted for the one-two punch: liners made by a company called Injinji, combined with merino wool socks from Darn Tough.

As a final protection, we lubricated our feet each morning to keep the skin from drying out and chafing. Vaseline will work for this purpose but leaves a disagreeable residue on the socks. Bina chose a roll-on product called Footglide, which she picked up at REI. I ordered a couple of tubes of HikeGoo from Amazon, based on some recommendations I had read. Both worked fine. The key point is that everyone's feet are different and you need to experiment.

The staff at Perimeter Atlanta's REI store got to know us well during this month of outfitting. It helped that some of them had walked the Camino themselves, such as Tom Beck. Now well into his middle 70s and known in the store as "Camino Tom," Beck continues to walk the Camino and gives periodic presentations on the topic.

With all that expert, in-store advice, bolstered by our own research, we loaded up on stuff both necessary and unnecessary.

The necessary included obvious things such as backpacks, shoes, light-weight shorts and dry-fast shirts and underwear.

The unnecessary included a $60 battery-powered probe light that you can strap to your forehead. Camino Tom said it would be useful when returning from dinner at night or when starting the trail in the pre-dawn hours. No doubt, he was right about that. But Bina and I never utilized the lamp for those purposes and it sat in my pack all the way from Porto to Santiago. At least it was not much larger than a golfball and weighed about as much.

More burdensome in the backpacks was all the rain gear we took, enough to cope with a flood of Biblical proportions: pants and jackets, dry gear bags, ponchos and backpack covers. We were lucky that we never had to pull them out. When we reached Santiago, we packed most of this stuff in a box and shipped it back to the States.

We were ready for rain but occasional fog and mist was the worst we encountered.

So, did we spend too much money on equipment? Can't deny it. On the other hand, all that rain gear would have come in handy if really needed. You could argue that preparing for the worst is a reasonable strategy. And we did get some things right, like that fast-dry underwear, which comes in very handy when you only take three each and have to wash them in the hotel sink nearly every night.[4]

---

1. As an example, Carolyn Train, a friend of Bina's, had her 2019 Camino plans derailed by Achilles tendinitis. She's now hoping to make the trip in 2020.
2. A blister prevention book that we found very helpful is *Fixing Your Feet: Injury Prevention and Treatments for Athletes* by John Vohhof.
3. Such as Wright socks, which Bina and I did experiment with. Some people swear by Wrights, which are double-lined. But for us, they didn't work so well on long distances.
4. We each actually took more than three pairs of underwear on the Camino, in our roller bags, but used the quick-dry ones exclusively on the trail. Our shirts and pants were likewise made of synthetic fabrics that dry overnight in hotel rooms.

5

CAMINO ON TRAINING WHEELS

Physical training constituted the final element in our Camino planning process. Bina and I had never undertaken any walk or physical exercise on this scale before, so we knew that we had to improve our conditioning before we arrived in Portugal.

We began this process in Costa Rica, where we lived from February to June 2018. For a few hours in the morning, several times a week, we walked the trails in a coffee farm located next to our rental apartment, which was situated on a ridge in the country's mountainous Central Valley. We had brought one set of trekking poles with us, to test them out. We discovered that using one pole each worked fine for us.

These walks at least got us started on the journey to improved conditioning. But it wasn't until we returned to Atlanta at the end of June that we were able to continue this training under more Camino-like conditions, with hiking shoes and backpacks.

The Airbnb basement apartment where we were staying at the time was situated near the Chattahoochee River, which features several national and state parks with hiking trails. After purchasing our equipment from REI, we began walking these

trails several times a week, boosting our kilometer count gradually from five to 12. It helped that Atlanta's bring-out-the-
sunscreen-and-sunglasses weather in early July replicated the
toasty conditions that we would encounter in Portugal.

Twelve kilometers admittedly represented a modest distance
compared to the 20 km-plus stretches we knew we would
encounter later on the Camino. Yet, the walks also helped us to
break in our new shoes and become accustomed to walking with
backpacks, which need to be strapped on so that the weight
pushes down on your waist, not your shoulders or back. Modern
backpacks include a lot of little straps to adjust — pull here, pull
there — so it's not always easy to get this right.

Bina had the sense to get the REI salespeople to adjust her
pack for her in the store. To make the adjustments as accurate as
possible, the salespeople even inserted weights in the pack to
replicate the load that Bina could expect to carry on the trail. I
was still struggling with my pack by the time we got to Portugal
and it took several days of trail walking before I finally figured out
how to eliminate the strain on my shoulders.

We were pleased to find that the combination of foot creme,
Injinji liners and Darn Tough socks seemed to do the job in terms
of blister protection. On some of these Atlanta walks, however, I
did experience a strange, non-itchy rash above the sock line. I
shrugged it off as some kind of sunburn or heat irritation. It
wasn't until I experienced the same condition in our early walks
in Portugal that a Google search identified a likely cause: vasculi-
tis, or "golfer's rash."

This heat- and exercise-induced rash appears to be related to
aging blood vessels, as it is more common in people over 50.
Delving into social media, Bina found some posts from other
peregrinos complaining about the same problem and noted that
one of these people had been wearing Injinji liners. We adopted
this person's recommendation to cut the elastic bands at the top,
which made the liners fit more loosely around the ankles. While

the rash continued to appear throughout the rest of the trip, particularly on very hot days, it became less obvious from this point on.

By the time we arrived in Lisbon on July 27, Bina and I felt reasonably confident about our equipment and physical conditioning. But we also knew that we weren't ready to jump into the Camino river and start swimming, not just yet. So, we had devised an elaborate plan to ease ourselves into the walk, a strategy we termed "Camino on Training Wheels."

After a few days of touristing around Lisbon, we took the train to Porto, where we had rented an apartment for a month. Our idea was to utilize this apartment as a base to walk the initial five stages of the coastal route from Porto to Viana do Castelo (VdC), which is 70 km north of Porto and 40 km from the Spanish border.

For each of these five days, we planned to leave the apartment, walk the planned distance, and then return to the apartment in the evening by utilizing some form of public transport, such as bus, metro, train, taxi or Uber. A day or so later, we would go out again and repeat the pattern, until we reached VdC. At that point, we would give up the Porto base and do the rest of our Camino as most *peregrinos* did it, by walking from town to town until we got to Santiago de Compostela.

The purpose of this ease-into-it strategy was to give us more time to improve our conditioning and learn how to pace ourselves on the walk. What's an ideal distance? How often should we take breaks? What's the right amount of equipment and food to carry in our day packs?

Essentially, we wanted to get our Camino formula right before abandoning the comfortable apartment in Porto, where we could rest for a few days between walks while enjoying one of Portugal's most interesting and scenic cities.

The location of our Porto apartment helped to facilitate this plan, as it was situated near the city's Foz do Douro section. This is a curve of land to the west of the city center where the Douro River meets the Atlantic. From the apartment, we could walk down a hill to pick up a bus on the main coastal road heading north. Alternatively, we could grab another bus that took us to Porto's Casa da Música terminal, and then board the metro heading north up the coast. We could also easily take the bus from our area to the São Bento train station, in Porto's city center, with its direct connection to Viana do Castelo.

Trouble is, having never set foot in Portugal before, we had no way of knowing how this plan to use public transport to move up and down the coast might work out in practice, as opposed to theory. Despite some diligent research, we couldn't find examples of other people doing this, at least not all the way to Viana do Castelo. So, there was no model to follow.

The strategy made sense to us at the time, but we couldn't be sure if it would work until we actually tried it.[1]

---

1. Spoiler alert: we would have been better off commencing the town-to-town walk earlier — for example, at Póvoa de Varzim (30 km from Porto), rather than at VdC. Póvoa, where the metro line from Porto ends, proved to be the last really convenient place to undertake all that to-ing and fro-ing along the coast.

6

STARTING OUT

After all the planning comes the day when you finally get to put it all into practice. For us, that was Monday, August 6. We left the apartment shortly after 8:30 a.m. and rode the bus into Porto's city center. Disembarking in front of the São Bento train station, we made a right turn to walk the short distance to the plaza on which sits the Sé do Porto, the city's grand Romanesque cathedral.

This is the most popular spot for starting the *Camino Portugues*. A couple of days previously, we had stopped at the table just inside the entrance to obtain our *Credencials del Peregrino*, or Pilgrim Passports, which already contained our first *sello* (stamp). It showed the cathedral coat of arms with the inscription around the circumference: "Fabrica da Catedral do Porto." Upon returning to the cathedral this morning, around 9:30, we went back in and asked the attendant to date and sign the stamp so it would show our starting date.

Outside, several groups of people with backpacks and trekking poles milled about the entrance taking photos of each other before heading off to Santiago de Compostela. We were about to pull out the selfie stick we had purchased a few days before when we noticed two young Dutch men standing nearby. Why not ask them to take the photo, in exchange for returning the favor? They were quite agreeable and we gave Bina's iPhone to one of them, who identified himself as Jacob. We smiled happily as he took the shot.

In our haste to get started on our Camino, Bina put away her iPhone, and away we went. Later that day, when we finally looked at the photo, we discovered that Jacob had pressed the button at the very moment when both of us had blinked. So, there we are, ready to embark upon our 200-mile adventure with our eyes closed. Bina had some fun with the situation in her trip blog by stating that the photo showed us "praying at the start of our Camino."

In any case, lesson learned. Next time, when you want to get a photo right, either check it right then or just use the selfie stick.

Preparing to embark upon the Camino with our eyes closed!

Otherwise, It proved an auspicious morning to commence our walk. For the past several days, searing winds from Africa had kept Portugal sweltering in a 90 plus degree sauna, keeping us grounded in our Porto apartment. Today, cooling Atlantic breezes had finally broken the heat wave.

The collision of these breezes with the lingering African heat had generated pea soup fog during the night and the sky remained hazy this morning, protecting us from the direct sunlight that can be so intense in Portugal this time of year. My Weather Channel app reported a pleasant 66 degrees and promised daytime highs no worse than the mid 70s. That was welcome news because we knew that little shade would be found during the day's walk to Matosinhos, a town 13 km up the coast from the Porto cathedral.

This cathedral sits on a hill overlooking the Douro River. To begin the walk, we would need to follow some twisty-turny paths down the hill to the esplanade running alongside the river. The *Wisely Pilgrim* app immediately made itself useful because the signage proved confusing. Just a few yards below the cathedral, we found one yellow arrow pointing to the left and another to the right. Is there a correct answer here, or does it not matter? *Wisely* instructed us to turn left and so we did, descending some narrow lanes to the Cais da Ribeira.

This is a section of the coastal esplanade very popular with tourists, since it offers sweeping views of the river and is adjacent to a bridge that connects Porto with the town of Vila Nova de Gaia on the other side. Nova de Gaia is where Porto wine merchants have traditionally maintained their storage cellars and where tourists go for port wine tastings. From noon on, Cais da Ribeira is typically shoulder-to-shoulder with tourists. But this early in the day, the restaurant and bar staff were just beginning to set out their tables and chairs for lunch.

From here, we turned right and followed the river west to where it empties into the Atlantic at Foz do Douro, effectively reversing our morning's bus ride from the apartment. Keeping our eyes focused on the river to our left helped us to ignore the clamorous city traffic to our right.

Reaching the park-like esplanade of Foz do Douro around 11, we stopped at the Douro Chique cafe for a break. Ordering an omelette for Bina and a grilled ham and cheese sandwich for me, we sipped our coffee at a tiny table at the water's edge and enjoyed the tranquility of the spot, watching some small boats plying about on the river.

Pleasantly fortified, we resumed our sauntering to the break-water that marks the mouth of the Douro. From there, we turned northward up the Atlantic coast, passing by a traffic circle surrounding São João Baptista, a well-preserved fort dating from the late 16th century. As we moved up the coast, we found an abundance of such fortifications, highlighting Portugal's efforts to preserve its independence in a period of intensifying conflict between the great European maritime powers.

This part of the Foz do Douro, with its parks, restaurants and cafes, is a popular entertainment spot for Porto urbanites. It also features a few small beaches among the rocks for sunbathers to stretch out and a few brave swimmers to dare the chilly Atlantic. This being August, those beaches were well-populated, even on a weekday.

Porto is the second largest city in Portugal (pop. 1.3 million), with suburban development that stretches up the coast almost to Matosinhos amid some quiet, park-like interludes. Fortunately for *peregrinos*, the stone-paved esplanade extends most of the way to Matosinhos so you can keep off the highway as you head north.

Just past a large traffic circle known as the Praça de Gonçalves Zarco, we passed another one of those 16th-17th century forts, the Castelo do Queijo, and then came upon the huge sprawl of the Matosinhos beach. This goes on for several kilometers until terminating at the cruise ship terminal near the entrance to the Leça River and the city's port facilities.

By now, it was after 2 p.m. and we were glad to be reaching the end of the day's walk. The sun, after hiding in the haze for much of the day, had finally begun to make its presence felt. Most of the walk along Matosinhos beach took place in the open, with no shade at all. While somewhat unpleasant for us, trudging along with our backpacks, the sun's return had lured some tourists in bathing suits onto the beach or to browse among the cafes and shops.

Contrasting oddly with this holiday scene was a grouping of stone sculptures portraying five women wailing with grief and throwing their arms out towards the sea. This display, set on the shoreline overlooking the beach, commemorates a 1947 storm in which 152 sailors lost their lives, a reminder of the harsh life of Portuguese fishermen on this coast just a generation ago.

Once past the beach, we ducked into a tourist information office to get the all-important stamp in our credentials booklets to prove that we had indeed reached Matosinhos. A short walk through town brought us to the bus terminal next to the central *mercado* (market) near the bridge (Ponte Movel) crossing the Leça River. This would be the spot where we would need to resume our walk, two days later. The entire day's 13 km saunter (precisely recorded on my MapMyWalk app), had taken us just under five hours, which included several rest stops along the way.

We then took the number 500 bus back Foz do Douro and our apartment, arriving in plenty of time to go shopping at a nearby grocery store, prepare dinner and relax for the evening. The first day of our Camino had gone well, leaving us feeling good about our Porto base plan and eager to have another go at it.

7

SCENE OF THE CRIME

For our next venture out, on Wednesday, we left the apartment around 8:30 a.m., walked down the hill to the bus stop and caught number 500 bus back to the central *mercado* in Matosinhos, where we had stopped two days before.

Hoisting our packs after exiting the bus, we climbed the nearby stairs of the Ponte Movel and crossed the Leça River on the pedestrian walkway. Turning left after the bridge, we covered the short distance through a neighborhood called Leça de Palmeira — much quieter than the main town of Matosinhos, on the other side of the river. At the waterfront esplanade, we turned north and headed up the Atlantic coast. The distance from here to our destination in the fishing town of Vila Cha was 15 km, only a few kilometers more than our first walk to Matosinhos.

Our spirits soared once we passed the vacation condos and apartments on the outskirts of Leça de Palmeira. The morning weather was delightful, mid-60s, and we now walked by long stretches of empty beach and brambly coastal vegetation spotted with clumps of white and yellow wildflowers. This was more in line with our image of how the Camino *should* feel.

We still had the occasional distraction of a car or truck

passing by on the highway to the right. But most of our attention could be focused to the left, where the waves crashed on the rocks in a shower of salt spray and the wide ocean horizon beckoned.

About four kilometers up the esplanade, we reached the Boa Nova lighthouse. Just past it, we found a small chapel perched on a hill overlooking the ocean. In the shelter of the rocks behind the chapel, we sat down to snack on cheese, sausage, cherries and nuts while looking out to the Atlantic. We could glimpse an occasional ship on the horizon as the sea breeze caressed our faces. Good place for a nap, had we been so inclined.

After the chapel, we had the opportunity to use the long stretches of beachfront boardwalk for which the coastal Portuguese Camino is famous. The elevation of the wooden pathway provides a better view of the ocean over the dunes. It also exposes you to a more unobstructed sea breeze, which was welcome on days like today, when the sun bore down from a mostly clear sky.

"It's like God turned on his air conditioning for us!" Bina exclaimed, coining a phrase that we would use often in the weeks ahead.

Love those boardwalks.

Continuing along the boardwalk for another four kilometers, we reached a memorial obelisk commemorating an event from the Portuguese civil war of 1828-34, which involved an extremely complex dispute over the royal succession. Suffice to say that forces belonging to the future king Dom Pedro IV landed success-fully on this beach in 1832 to capture Porto and further his cause in the war.

More history awaited in our approach to the fishing village of Angeiras, where we came upon a fence enclosing several square holes in the ground lined with bricks. Stopping to read the plaques, which included an English translation, we learned that these structures dated from Roman times, when the people salted fish to produce the perky fermented *garum* sauce. In an age when access to spices was very limited (pepper imported from

India was available only to the very rich), the Romans relied on *garum* to season their otherwise bland food.

In Angeiras itself, we encountered tourist-packed streets and smoke from outdoor grills set up on the sidewalks by the numerous restaurants. It was now close to 2 p.m., prime lunchtime for the Portuguese. With the smells so tempting, we couldn't resist stopping at one of these establishments, where we treated ourselves to grilled sea bass served with grilled vegetables and roasted potatoes. We left about 45 minutes later, pleasantly satiated. Actually, too satiated.

"Oh boy, I don't know if eating all that food was a good idea," I commented, as we trudged the final four kilometers to Vila Chã under a still-broiling sun.

Bina grimaced in agreement. "What were we thinking of?"

We had been thinking we were hungry. Yet, as we now realized, splurging on a full meal in a sit-down restaurant can be counter-productive when you're walking the Camino, particularly on a hot day.

It would have been better to grab something lighter and faster, such as a sandwich or salad, and then gotten back on the trail. But that's hard to do in Spain and Portugal, where your options are typically limited to sit-down restaurants of the kind we had just visited; cafes that primarily serve coffee and snacks; and bakeries, where it's all sugar and carbs, which Bina can't tolerate because of her diabetes.

After passing through one more fishing town, Labruge, we finally reached Vila Chã, happy to call it a day. We parked ourselves at the Cafe Praia Mar to use the restroom and call Uber. The Metro line from Porto maintained a few stops to the east of Vila Chã and Google Maps told us that we were only about 20 minutes by car from the closest one, located by an outlet mall near the town of Modivas.

Taking the metro seemed like a more comfortable and faster way to get back to Porto than trying to find a bus back to

Matosinhos and from there to Porto. Unfortunately, when Bina checked her Uber app, she couldn't find an available car — no surprise, since Vila Chã is a small place. It appeared that our only option was to call a taxi, not good news.

With Uber, everything is automated in the app: the pickup time and destination, the identity of the driver and his vehicle and the payment itself. To call a taxi in a foreign country is more difficult. For starters, which taxi service serves your particular area? You can try Googling for a few names. But then you have to call a dispatcher (who likely doesn't speak English), try to describe the pickup and destination points (more language hassles) and then worry about whether the driver will try to cheat you by taking you the long way around.

Since arriving in Portugal, we had been delighted to discover that Uber is easily accessible in major cities, such as Lisbon and Porto. It proved a different story out here in the countryside, however.

I went into the cafe to ask the woman behind the bar to call us a taxi. She would know whom to call locally and provide proper location information to the dispatcher. It took a while to get her attention, since the bar was crowded with locals, but I finally communicated my request and walked back outside to join Bina at the table. The 15 minutes the woman at the bar had promised me stretched into half an hour and we got impatient. We quizzed a passing waiter, who offered a general assurance of "soon."

It was now around 4:30 and Bina went back to checking her Uber app. Lo and behold, the screen suddenly showed a driver in the area, about 15 minutes away. What should we do?

The people at the cafe had been kind enough to call us a taxi. We would leave them facing an angry driver if we grabbed Uber instead. But how much longer would we find ourselves sitting at that cafe? And Uber was soooo much more convenient. Oh, the hell with it.

Bina pressed the request-car button on her Uber app and I went back into the cafe to explain that we no longer needed a taxi. The *barrista* was quite put out, protesting that the taxi would soon arrive. I said sorry, as best I could in Portuguese, and retreated back to the table, where we shouldered our packs and set off down the street.

The Uber driver picked us up in full view of the cafe, where the taxi driver arrived at the same time to pick up his fare, now nearly 45 minutes after he had been summoned. Bina and I studiously looked the other way as we drove past the scene of the crime. We felt bad that we had put the cafe to all that trouble and only purchased two cups of coffee.

The Uber driver dropped us off at the outlet mall, a modern retail complex. At the adjacent metro stop, we caught a very comfortable and clean train back to Porto's Casa da Música station, which is named for the nearby concert hall. An escalator at Casa da Música carried us up to the bus terminal at street level, where we found the line that serviced our neighborhood in Foz do Douro.

Switching between metro and bus in Porto's transportation system is easy because both use the same fare card, which you electronically swipe when you board. We were back at our apartment by 6:15 p.m., just in time to shower and change and go have dinner at a nearby restaurant on the riverfront.

So far, the return-to-Porto strategy was working pretty well.

8

NOT A ROMAN AQUEDUCT

T he next day, we did the Vila Chã-to-Porto trip in reverse. Leaving our apartment at 8:15 a.m., we took the number 504 bus to Casa da Música, where we caught the metro back to the outlet mall. Disembarking there at 9:15, we called Uber and asked the driver to drop us off near the cafe we had left so abruptly the previous day.

Such precision was necessary because Bina and I were determined to walk the Camino without "cheating" — in other words, without skipping any stages in the official path. It would have been easy to do that. Don't like a section? Just Uber or taxi through it. Nobody at the pilgrims office in Santiago would have been the wiser, as long as we acquired the requisite stamps in our credentials book along the way.

Still, we preferred to keep this Camino experience as authentic as possible, which meant walking the full 300 plus km to the cathedral in Santiago de Compostela in a point-to-point manner.

Today, we planned to cover about 19 km to the large coastal town of Póvoa de Varzim. Since the metro line from Porto terminated there, we anticipated an easy ride back to our apartment at the end of the walk.

When we set off from Vila Chã at 9:45, the temperature was a comfortable 63 degrees and not expected to rise above 70 in the afternoon, normally an ideal day. The winds from the Atlantic, however, kicked up gradually throughout the day, from 5 mph when we started, to 22 by the time we finished at 4:15 p.m. That made this day's Camino segment more challenging than the previous two.

Initially, we walked along coastal boardwalks before deviating inland, passing from one urban area after another: Gafa, Avore, Azurara, Vila do Conde and Póvoa de Varzim. Most of these places were charming in their own way, with old churches, blue and white tile signs and sidewalk cafes.

The fact that much of this section of the trail took us through cobblestone streets did put Bina's Hoka One One trail runners at a disadvantage. She felt every bump. Whenever possible, she walked on sidewalks or level dirt besides the road. Some of the villages had lanes paved down the middle with larger stone squares, rather than cobblestones, which provided Bina a smoother path. The houses and walls of the towns also helped shield us from the wind, which we appreciated more as the day wore on.

Soon after leaving Vila Chã we experienced some confusion when we entered a patch of scrubby pine forest (later determined to be a bird sanctuary), where the paved sidewalk quickly devolved into a sand-and-dirt path. Other dirt paths branched off from this one and the *Wisely Pilgrim* app wasn't clear about which one to take.

This area also lacked any yellow arrows or Camino scallop signs to guide us. The reason for this is that we had decided to walk the *Senda Litoral*, a variant of the coastal route that keeps you closer to the coast but isn't as well marked. A few times we set off down a path only to backtrack when we realized that we had made the wrong choice.

As a last resort, we just stuck with a track broader than the others that appeared to be heading in the right general direction, northward, toward the town of Avore. Having guessed right, we entered Avore and then continued on to another small town, Azurara. There, we sat down on the shaded steps of the Santa Maria church to eat our day's snack of cheese, sausage and carrots.

When we reached the Ave River, we crossed the bridge to Vila do Conde. This small city, a cluster of white buildings with pink-tiled roofs, had earned fame as a major port during Portugal's Age of Discovery in the 15th and 16th century centuries. Now, it's one of the most popular tourist destinations on the country's northern coast, appreciated both for its beaches and its historical charm.

The northern bank, as you view it from the bridge, is dominated by the fortress-like walls of the Convent of Santa Clara, which dates back to the 16th century. This enormous hulk of a building — greatly expanded in the 18th century — became so wealthy that benefactors built an aqueduct to supply its water needs.

Seeing the ruins of the arches and water channel from a distance, I wondered to myself, "Could that be Roman?" The Romans, after all, built aqueducts all over Europe, such as the Pont du Gard in France. A later Google search revealed that lots of European cities built aqueducts between the 16th and 19th centuries using the old Roman model.

Turning left along the Vila do Conde waterfront and then climbing the hill to the city center, we found a tourist office for the all-important *sellos* (stamps) in our credentials book. After a cup of coffee at a cafe across the street, we walked back down the hill to the waterfront park, where a replica of a 16th century *carrack* rested at anchor. This is the type of ship the Portuguese used to explore Africa and India back in the days when the country led the world in maritime riches.

We would have liked to have spent more time exploring this charming town but it was now late afternoon and we wanted to get back to Porto before dark. So, after promising ourselves that we would return to spend more time in Vila do Conde at a later time, continued the final four kilometers up the coast to Póvoa de Varzim, which is best known for its white sandy beaches and modern condo developments. The metro line from Porto terminates here so the town is flooded with Portuguese beach-goers in the summer.

We halted our walk for the day at the Barracuda Mar restaurant overlooking the beach, then tried to call Uber for the ride to the metro station. We were amazed to discover that Póvoa lacked any Uber drivers, despite the town's size, so we had to ask the staff in the Barracuda Mar to call us a taxi. Luckily this one arrived quickly. We reached the metro station by 5 p.m., for another easy ride back to Porto.

This had been the longest of the three days of walking that we had done so far, both in terms of distance (nearly 20 km) and hours spent on the trail. All that walking had left us tired, to be sure, but not excessively so, with no signs of blisters or other foot problems. We returned to Porto with a surge of confidence in our ability to handle the Camino.

"Today makes me feel like we can do this!" Bina said to me, as we waited to board the metro.

We did this walk to Póvoa on a Thursday, August 9. Knowing that Portuguese public transport maintained less frequent schedules on weekends, we had already decided to wait until the following Monday to resume our Camino. That left us three days to run errands in Porto and engage in some touristic activities, such as a train excursion up the Douro Valley to see the vineyards around Pinhão.

We also had time to re-think our current schedule, which

included two more Camino segments before we finally left the Porto apartment for Viana do Castelo on Tuesday, August 21. We now decided to move that departure up by two days, to Sunday the 19th.

To be sure, we enjoyed hanging around Porto, which is one of the most interesting cities in Portugal, full of historic churches and other buildings decorated with the country's famous blue *azulejo* ceramic tiles. And we found our apartment quite comfortable, with a grocery store just around the corner and good restaurants a short walk away by the waterfront.

Yet, walking the Camino had been the most fun we had had so far in Portugal and we wanted to jump deeper into that experience. There's the sense of anticipation you get when hitting the trail each morning with the promise of adventure ahead. The scenery, whether coastal vistas or medieval towns, presents a continual feast for the eyes while the act of walking itself pumps blood into your brain and makes you feel more alive.

Our landlady was okay with us leaving the apartment early and even graciously refunded the last two days of rent. The challenge was revising our entire itinerary of accommodations on booking.com to facilitate the new accelerated schedule.

Fortunately, we had taken the precaution of reserving only those places that offered "free cancellation," usually up to two or three days before our scheduled arrival. That gave us just enough leeway to cancel bookings and insert new ones, although we did end up with some less-than-ideal selections. For Viana do Castelo itself, for example, we had to book a place located a good five kilometers south of town, which we knew would present some logistical complications.

But, we took what we could get, since the August beach-goers seemed to be inundating northern Portugal. We had been noticing anguished posts popping up in the *Camino de Santiago Forum* from *peregrinos* complaining about finding no room at the inn when they reached their planned destinations for the day.

We didn't want to find ourselves in that situation so we made sure to book ahead.

9

THE DELICACY OF TRIPE

Our next two Camino segments, which took us up to Viana do Castelo, would drive home for us the diminishing appeal of the return-to-Porto strategy.

We got an early taste of this on August 13, when we boarded the 504 bus near our apartment at 7:30 a.m. and caught the eight o'clock metro to Póvoa de Varzim, arriving 40 minutes later. Grabbing a taxi at the metro station, we disembarked near the Póvoa waterfront at 8:50.

Thus, it took nearly an hour and a half between leaving our apartment and resuming the walk. For our return that afternoon, from Esposende, we boarded a bus at 3:55 p.m., reached the Póvoa metro station by 4:40, then caught the train to Porto five minutes later. It was 6 p.m. by the time the bus dropped us back at the apartment. Altogether, it took us two hours to get back to Porto, nearly four hours total transitioning between apartment and Camino that day!

Adding insult to injury, we didn't even start the day's walk at the same place we had left off four days before. When we picked up the taxi at the Póvoa metro station, we asked the driver to drop us off at the Barracuda Mar restaurant on the waterfront. Something got lost in translation, however, because he stopped a kilometer short of the restaurant, which we didn't realize until we got out of the car.

Such a mistake would not have occurred with Uber, by the way, because your destination is always clearly shown on the app. We spent an extra 20 minutes retracing our steps to the restaurant, which is located on a beach called A Ver-o-Mar, on the northern outskirts of Póvoa.

Despite this minor mishap, a glorious sunny sky and comfortable temperature of 66 degrees beckoned us back to the Camino. Once we passed the last condo and apartment blocks of Póvoa, we found ourselves traversing quiet beaches on the elevated wooden boardwalks that we had become so fond of. There's something quite calming about seeing a mostly deserted coastline stretch out before you. We encountered only a few fellow *peregrinos* on the trail and occasional locals fishing in the surf or gathering seaweed. Seaweed?

So much seaweed is deposited on the beaches of northern Portugal that some locals take the time to rake it up and bundle it into large bales. After the bundles have dried, they hire trucks to transport the bales to factories that process the seaweed into fertilizer. Until the advent of mass tourism in the 1960s, harvesting this variety of seaweed, known as *sargaço*, had been a major industry for poor families along this part of the coast. Today, only a few older people still carry on the tradition.

By the looks of it, much more money comes into the local economy from tourism, which has rejuvenated beachfront towns all along the northern coast of Portugal. Vegetable gardening is also big in this area, despite the sandy soil. Once the trail took us away from the beach to the main coastal road, we passed a succession of large greenhouses featuring cabbages, water melons, lettuce and leeks.

We also noticed a lot of corn fields, which puzzled us. Corn did not seem to figure prominently in the Portuguese diet. You never saw it in restaurants and only occasionally in grocery stores. We later learned that this corn is mostly grown for animal feed, not human consumption.

On the outskirts of the small town of Aguçádoura, the *Wisely* app presented us with a choice: continue with the official route, which ran slightly inland, or branch off onto a *Senda Litoral* path closer to the coast. We opted for the second, thinking it would be more scenic and provide access to the sea breezes, or "God's air conditioning." The afternoon heat had reached the mid-70s and was still rising.

It wasn't long, however, before the gravel-packed trail petered out into deep sand that grabbed at every footfall. By the time we reached the beachside town of Apúlia, Bina had to sit down on a low wall overlooking the beach and shake the sand from her shoes, which rode lower on the ankles than mine. I sat down besides her and we consumed our usual sausage-and-cheese snack.

The Apúlia beachfront proved a good spot to relax, as we idly watched the boys playing soccer in the sand, Portuguese families strolling about and dark-skinned gypsies selling clothes and household items from their carts lined up along the esplanade. Further on, past the public beach, we encountered cylindrical stone towers with pointed roofs. These were former windmills that had been restored to provide rent-able accommodations, with great views of the coastline from the upper floors.

After Apúlia, the coastal road parallels the beach for a while before turning inland to the town of Fão, which is located across the Rio Cávado from the large resort town of Esposende. Crossing the river required walking across a long two-lane highway bridge with narrow pedestrian catwalks on each side. This proved a bit harrowing, with the wind beating against us and the water a long drop down.

"I ... don't ... like .... this ...." Bina said, through gritted teeth, as she edged forward. Like her, I reached for the railings with every step and tried to avoid looking down.

Glad to reach the other side, we walked through a park into the center of Esposende, where we found a chapel dedicated to Santiago (St. James). A stamp for imprinting a *sello* had been conveniently left on a table inside.

Then we considered the pressing issue of lunch, since the benefits of our snack back at Apúlia beach had worn off. Not finding anything but cafes in the center of town, I suggested retracing our steps to a restaurant I had noticed shortly after crossing the river. It had been full of diners at that time, which is usually a good sign. It had even advertised some kind of stew as the "Menu do Peregrino." But when we returned, at 3 p.m., the restaurant was mostly empty, the tables still cluttered with dirty dishes.

The man tending the bar, who spoke only broken English, identified the one meal available as a "bean stew," which sounded hearty enough. This turned out to be *dobrada guisada*. Also known as *Tripas a Moda do Porto* (Porto style tripe), this is a popular dish in Portugal. We were willing to give it a try, despite knowing that the main ingredient is cow intestines. Hey, even the French eat tripe, so it must be some kind of delicacy, right?

Bina, sensibly, ate only a small portion whereas my larger appetite required a bowl and a half. Served me right. For the rest of that hot afternoon, my stomach turned over uneasily, as if complaining, "Now, why did you do that to me?" For days afterward, Bina took the lead in suggesting places to eat.

After lunch, we dragged ourselves to the tourist office near the waterfront, where we obtained the schedules for the Minho Bus Company, which served this part of the coast. A woman behind the counter gave us directions to the nearest stop to catch the next scheduled bus back to Póvoa de Varzim. To Bina's delight, this turned out to be an English-like double decker, which she hadn't ridden on since her childhood days back in

Bombay, India. We sat up top, in the very front, and enjoyed the view all the way back to the Póvoa metro station.

We were seriously dragging by the time we reached our apartment that evening. The 19 km walk, combined with four hours transitioning between Porto and the Camino, had been too much. We decided to take three days off before returning to Esposende to embark upon the final leg to Viana do Castelo.

10

PARTY CITY

F or the last segment of our Camino using Porto as a base, on August 17, we decided to make it easy on ourselves.

From our experience four days earlier, we knew that utilizing public transportation to return to Esposende would take two hours or more. We also estimated that the subsequent walk from Esposende to Viana do Castelo would cover about 28 km, a longer distance than usual for us.

Given those factors, it made sense to start the walk early and avoid as much of the afternoon heat as possible. That left only one sensible option: take Uber.

Waking up at 5:45 that morning, we had breakfast and were standing outside our apartment building by 7:30. Bina immediately found an Uber driver on her app. He showed up in a few minutes later in a comfortable, late model Renault to take us up the coast back to the bus stop on the Esposende esplanade. The ride cost us $50, but we covered the 50 km to Esposende in less than half the time it would have taken using bus and metro.

Resuming our Camino at 8:30, we continued north along the lovely Esposende esplanade, which includes both pedestrian and bicycle paths. At the northern outskirts, we turned inland and left the beaches behind, entering a terrain that more closely resembled what I imagined the interior Portuguese Camino to be like: one small town after another, with stretches of woodland in between.

In the area known as Antas, between Belinho and Castelo do Neiva, we followed the boulder-strewn trail up a ridge line. Descending at the other end, we reached a stone pedestrian bridge, the Ponte do Sebastião, and crossed the small Neiva river, passing a gentle waterfall on the right. We both paused on the bridge to hold hands. The Camino was made for moments like this. Bina took a video capturing the sounds of the waterfall to enjoy again at a later time.

In the town of Castelo do Neiva, on the other bank, we found a church that dated back to 862 dedicated to Santiago (St. James). As the front door was open, we wandered inside and were delighted to find a table with the ink pad and stamp needed to provide the day's *sello* for our credential booklets. The administrators or members of this church had even been thoughtful enough to provide a few cookies for *peregrinos* like us to snack on.

Continuing on through another wooded section, our route took us down a country lane hedged on each side by stone walls of local farms. There, we began to pay attention to a bell tinkling. "Where's *that* coming from?" Bina asked me.

"No idea, I've been wondering myself," I responded. "It seems to be somewhere ahead of us."

The bell also seemed to move with us as we walked. Could there be a *peregrino* ahead of us with a bell-like ring tone on his cell phone? If so, why didn't he or she answer the damn phone?

"Can it be angels' bells?" Bina asked, maybe only half in jest. "This is the Camino de Santiago, after all!"

Finally, we turned a bend and found the answer: a bell hung from the neck of a goat walking along the top of the wall to our right. Either picking up our scent or hearing the crunching of our shoes on the trail, the animal had been judiciously keeping its distance. Now, with us in full view, the goat scooted along at a quickened pace, the bell tinkling merrily.

Hoping to get a photo on my smart phone, I rushed to keep up, trying not to make too much noise clomping down the path. Suddenly, I stopped at the sight of a baby goat standing in the path ahead, eying me uncertainly. As the mother bleated, the baby poised itself and jumped on the wall to join her. Just as I was positioning myself to snap some photos of the pair, they both leaped off the wall and disappeared on the other side.

Maybe the Camino was trying to teach me to just enjoy the moment instead of trying to capture everything on my iPhone?

We emerged from the woods at the monastery of São Romão de Neiva, which is perched on a hill overlooking the town of Alvarães in the valley below. We would have liked to take a peek inside the church, but found the doors locked.

From here, we crossed mostly open terrain on country roads that took us past scattered farm houses and into the small town of Chafé. The afternoon sun now beginning to make its presence felt, we stopped at a small park and took off our socks and shoes to air out our feet. Somewhat refreshed by this pause, we proceeded on to the next town of Anha, found a cafe near the main church, and contemplated our situation.

The *Wisely* app reported another 5.5 km to Viana do Costelo, where we planned to pick up the train to take us back to Porto. That distance normally entailed about an hour and a half of walking, which we thought we could handle.

But we didn't really have to continue on the Viana because Anha was actually the spot where we would resume the next leg of our Camino in three days' time. Since all the good accommodations in Viana itself had been booked, we had reserved a guesthouse right here, called Dias House. There was no reason why we couldn't just call it a day and grab Uber or a taxi to zip us on up to the Viana train station.

We definitely considered that option because we were already tired enough from walking nearly 23 km in the last six and a half hours. Small problem: Bina could not find any Uber in this area, so that meant taking a taxi. However, we had not seen a single taxi since we had entered Anha. We could have asked the cafe owner to try to call one, but we had already noticed that he spoke no English and wasn't particularly friendly to begin with. We also knew, from previous experience, that we could sit there a long time waiting for a taxi to show up.

"Do you think you can handle the walk into Viana?" I asked Bina.

"Yeah, I think so. What about you?"

"I'm okay. There's still plenty of time to catch the train back to Porto, since they run nearly every hour into the late evening. Let's just do it."

Hoisting our backpacks, we set off down the road again. We began to question our decision almost immediately. The Camino "trail" to Viana took us along a major highway, never a comfortable walk, with the cars whizzing by uncomfortably close. The terrain was also hillier than expected. And the road offered little shade in the 80 degree heat. We looked for taxis to flag down as we walked but saw none. We felt quite bedraggled by the time we reached the long bridge that crosses the Lima river into Viana.

Just before crossing the bridge, we passed a storefront where two women, city employees in blue shirts, were handing out leaflets to passers-by. What's up with that? We stopped to chat, mainly to ascertain the best route to the train station.

A young woman who spoke English showed me a map of Viana and explained how to navigate to the station. Then, I casually asked her why we were seeing so many cars driving past us into Viana. I had noticed the traffic backing up from the bridge to this side of the river. Since it was now past 4 p.m., I assumed that these cars represented the beginning of rush hour. But why were they driving *into* Viana rather than out of it?

"Oh, don't you know?" she replied. "There's a big festival this weekend."

Say what?

"Yes," she continued brightly. "Today is the start of the *Romaria de Nossa Senhora da Agonia* (Festival of our Lady of the Agony), our biggest festival of the year. People come from all over northern Portugal, including Porto. It will last until Monday."

Bina and I exchanged desolate looks. All we wanted to do at that point was to grab a quick bite to eat in Viana and then settle into a comfortable train ride back to Porto. Now, we faced at least another half hour of trudging across that bridge into a city whose streets would be jammed with thousands of festival goers. And what if the train schedules had been disrupted? Could we even get a seat?

Bina and I had enjoyed many nice bonding moments during our Camino, such as the pause on the bridge earlier in the day. We had also experienced some tensions, inevitable in travel, when things went wrong. In this case, Bina wanted to know: why hadn't I researched Portuguese festivals sufficiently to avoid this mess? And for crying out loud, how had I missed the biggest festival of the whole damned year?

But, but, but ....

In truth, we should have been on our guard. Two days before, we had packed a box of excess gear to send ahead to Santiago de Compostela. I had taken it by bus from our Porto apartment to the post office only to discover the office closed for Assumption of Mary Day. That holiday commemorates Mary, the mother of Jesus, being taken up to heaven upon her death. It is celebrated every August 15 in most Catholic countries.

Forced to repeat the trip the next day, I subsequently compiled a list of all national Portuguese and Spanish holidays in my iPhone's Notes file. What I had not thought to do was add a list of *local* festivals and holidays for all the cities that we would pass through. As we would discover repeatedly on this trip, nearly every place of habitation on the Iberian Peninsula hosts some festival during the year to celebrate their local saint or some historical event.

Recriminations aside, we had to make a decision. Theoretically, we could find a bus stop and try to catch a regional bus back to Póvoa de Varzim, from where we could take the metro back to Porto. But we had no idea of the bus schedules, which might be disrupted in any case by all the traffic in Viana.

The best bet still seemed to reach the Viana station to catch one of the trains back to Porto. Any way you looked at it, the train would provide the fastest way back. On the downside, we would have zero chance of finding accommodations in Viana that evening if the trains were full.

The trek across Viana's 19th century iron frame bridge, the *Pont Eiffel* (yes, that Eiffel), confirmed our worst fears. Vehicular traffic had slowed to a crawl as irritable motorists honked their horns. Once in the city, we got swallowed up in crowds of people brandishing plastic cups or beer bottles. The density increased as we tried to maneuver our way toward the train station, which is in the center of the old town. The noise around us increased to the point where Bina and I had to shout at each other to communicate.

A few blocks from the station, a parade forming in the street stopped us cold, as women in traditional costume with lots of lace and gold jewelry chatted amongst themselves while a band tuned up. We took a few minutes to capture the scene on our cell cameras before resuming our glacial progress to the train station.

Getting ready to parade.

The crowds packing both sides of the street made it difficult for us to cross. Back and forth along the sidewalk we walked until we finally found enough room to elbow our way across and stumble into the train station at 5:30 p.m.

Here, we were pleasantly surprised to find the ticket line relatively short. We purchased two seats for the 6:48 to Porto, which left us just enough time to grab something to eat. But where? Every restaurant and fast-food eatery in Viana was mobbed. No way were we going to venture out into that chaos again, particularly with the bands playing and the parade beginning to snake through the streets. The only option was the train station's tiny cafe and bar, where we shared a microwaved pork cutlet sandwich, about the only thing on the menu, other than pastry.

About a quarter after 6, as we made our way back into the station to use the restrooms, we encountered a surge of people entering the building. The line at the women's restroom extended into the corridor.

"Should I try to go?" Bina asked, eying the line doubtfully. "There's usually a loo on the train so we can just use that."

Or, maybe not. It was more than an hour's ride back to Porto. And people were now packing the train platform *en masse*, signaling that a mad scramble to board lay ahead. Better to take care of business while we could. After quickly ducking into the men's room, I stood in the hallway and fumed with anxiety for 20 minutes while waiting for Bina to emerge from the ladies.' She finally did, with just minutes to spare before the train trundled into the station.

Our best hope of getting a seat depended on the train stopping with us positioned right in front of a door. No such luck. We tried to elbow our way on board with the best of them but found all the seats taken by the time we clambered up the steps into the car. All we could do was stand in the corridor as people wedged in tightly around us. We placed our backpacks at our feet to maintain a thinner profile in the crush of bodies. As the train shuddered out of the station, we could barely turn around.

Quickly, we became aware of another issue: the train's air conditioning lacked the power to cool this many people. Outside, the temperature still hovered in the low 80s and no breeze circulated.

Putting a final cap on our misery, Bina and I had been on our feet for nearly 10 hours and felt it. It wasn't until about half an hour into the ride that enough people exited at the towns we passed through to enable us to collapse into two seats.

"Have you been enjoying our wonderful festival?" a woman's voice asked, from across the aisle. I turned to look at a chirpy, black-haired young woman.

Her name was Sandra and she spoke excellent English, having spent some years working in London. She proceeded to explain to us how the people in northern Portugal loved festivals and took them very seriously, spending months on the preparation. That gold jewelry that we had seen on the women assembling for the parade? Much of it was real gold, traditional handiwork handed down from generation to generation.

"The women keep all those old necklaces and bracelets in chests in their homes and then bring them out on occasions liked this. They love to put on the old costumes and parade around in them once a year. It's just part of the culture here."

"People in northern Portugal have a reputation for being very cold and business-like," Sandra added, "particularly compared to those who live in the south, who are very excitable.

"But, people here are also very emotional under the surface. And you see that when we have our festivals. All that love comes out when they put on the traditional costumes."

It's unfortunate that Bina and I had failed to appreciate that love when we walked right into it. We had been so focused on just getting out of Viana. On this day, the logistics of travel had just wiped us out.

The train didn't pull into Porto's São Bento station until 8:30 and it was 9 p.m. by the time the the bus dropped us off near the apartment. We had essentially just spent a 12 and a half hour day, from the time we left the apartment in the morning until the time we got back.

Yes, it was now well past time to abandon our base in Porto.

11

THE REAL CAMINO

Following our return from Viana do Castelo, Bina and I spent the next day, Saturday, resting up in the Porto apartment and packing for our transfer the following day to the lodging near Viana. Beginning on Monday, August 20, we would start what we called our "real Camino," by walking north from town to town until we reached Santiago de Compostela.

Our original plan for Sunday had been to take the train back to Viana and then cab it from there to our lodging in Vila Nova d'Anha, a bed & breakfast called Dias House. However, the festival in Viana, which would continue through the entire weekend, put the kibosh on that. No way were we going to dump ourselves into that mess again. We decided to use Uber to go directly to the Dias House and then deal with Viana on Monday morning, when we hoped the festival would be winding down.

At 3 p.m., we left the apartment with all our luggage — two backpacks and two roller bags, way too much stuff! Bina found an Uber driver on the app and within five minutes a comfortable, late model, black Renault was conveying us over the 65 km to Dias House. We sustained another $50 charge to dent our budget.

But schlepping around with all that luggage on a train or bus would have made no sense. With the festival in full swing, we didn't even know if we could get a taxi to take us from the train station to our lodgings.

I had made the reservation for Dias House on booking.com and subsequently exchanged some emails with Narciso, the family's English-speaking son. Narciso was not in when we arrived, around 4. We were greeted instead by his elderly mother, who spoke only Portuguese and wore the black dress and sweater traditionally worn by older Portuguese women. She took us upstairs to show us our room, handed us the key, and left Bina and I to contemplate our next task, which was to find some dinner.

We had learned from past experience that restaurants in Portugal tend to close on Sunday. Narciso had told me in the earlier phone call that we could find a cafe near his house but he was not on hand to give us any directions. All that we could gather from fumbled attempts to communicate with his mother was that Narciso would show up sometime that evening.

Since no other guests were around to ask for advice, we consulted Google Maps, which identified two cafes — but no restaurants — within walking distance. This worried us because Portuguese cafes typically don't feature proper kitchens. You're lucky if you can buy a pastry or snack, which would not work with Bina's diabetes. She needed some kind of meat or fish for protein, hopefully accompanied by vegetables or a salad. In hindsight, we realized we should have planned ahead and just brought food with us from our Porto apartment!

The best we could do was something designated as a "hotdog" on the menu of the second of the two cafes we visited. This turned out to be cut-up sausage served between two slices of toast, instead of a hotdog bun. Back at the Dias House, we had to supplement this poor fare with some cheese we had brought from Porto, not a particularly satisfactory meal.

Fortunately, when we went downstairs for breakfast the next morning, we found that Narciso's mother had prepared a lush breakfast of scrambled eggs, bacon and fruit. Narciso himself showed up to check on things, which enabled us to explain our transportation issues.

The first had to do with luggage transfer. For the rest of the journey to Santiago, we had arranged for a company called Tuitrans to transport our two roller bags from lodging to lodging. This would enable us to conduct our walks with day packs only.

We had emailed Tuitrans our planned schedule so they knew where we would be each night. If the system worked as it was supposed to, their van would arrive later that morning to pick up the roller bags from Dias House. But Tuitrans had told us that we needed to make sure that someone, Narciso or his mother, would be on hand to let their people in through the compound gate, which was typically locked.

"Yes, we know how this process works," Narciso said. "We do this all the time so you should have no worries."

Good to know.

The second issue related to the starting point for the day's walk. We could have simply walked out of the Dias House and connected with the Camino trail half a kilometer away. However, that would have meant repeating the six kilometer walk from Anha to Viana do Castelo that we had made last Friday afternoon, a pointless (and tiring) exercise.

What we really needed was transport from the Dias House to the train station in Viana, where we had actually ended Friday's walk. Unfortunately, Uber was not available in the Anha area and all the local taxis appeared to be working the festival in Viana.

Narciso listened to our dilemma and said his father could drive us to the train station, for no charge. We gladly accepted the kind offer, although I did tip the father five euros for his troubles. Twenty minutes later, at quarter of nine, Bina and I found ourselves hoisting our packs in front of the Viana train station ready to resume our Camino.

The contrast with our last venture into Viana couldn't have been more dramatic. The plaza in front of the train station was nearly empty, except for us and a sculpture of a dancing couple in traditional costume. Rather apropos, considering the revelry of the previous couple of days. Only a few distant figures could be glimpsed further down the Avenida dos Combatentes de Grande Guerra, the boulevard leading to the waterfront. We assumed a lot of tourists were still sleeping off the previous night's partying, as testified by all the empty bottles and paper cups littering the streets.

As we walked down the Avenida, we could see evidence of locals getting ready for the festival's final day. On a side street by a church, for example, we found a high school band assembling with their instruments while costumed figures with enormous heads practiced their routines.

These tall figures, known as *Gigantones (Giants)* in Portuguese, are common to Portuguese and Spanish festivals. The men hidden underneath the costumes are actually standing at ground level controlling an aluminum frame that they move about via a shoulder harness. The frames are topped by heads made of *carton pierre*, a mixture of papier mâché and plaster of paris. In addition to simply entertaining the crowds, the *Gigantones* in this festival have a quasi-religious duty, which is to exorcise evil from the world.

Giants among men.

Viana's annual festival, which dates back to the 18th century, is dedicated to *Nossa Señora D'Agonia* (Our Lady of the Agony), a designation for the Virgin Mary, who is worshipped in this part of Portugal as the patron saint of fishermen. The seafaring aspect of the festival became more obvious as we continued down to the waterfront plaza, where craft and food booths were beginning to reopen for the day. Along with workers from the city, some vendors had taken up brooms to sweep up the trash around them.

Just beyond the plaza heading north, we found a most astonishing sight: narrow side lanes seemingly over laid with multicolored carpets featuring nautical and religious motifs. On closer examination, these "carpets" turned out to be made of colored gravel painstakingly poured and arranged on the streets. At the time we walked by, locals were still putting finishing touches to their creations.

Magic carpet ride.

Once we left the outskirts of Viana, our day's walk hugged the coast all the way to our destination of Vila Praia de Ancora (literally, "beach city of the Âncora River"). Very early on, we donned our floppy hats and sunglasses, as no clouds marred the pure blue of the sky. The temperature, in the low 70s when we left the train station, reached 84 by late afternoon. This was definitely a day when we were grateful for "God's air conditioning." But the scenery was worth it, as we strolled by a profusion of white buttercups and miles of coastal scrub blanketed in purple heather. A touch of Scotland in Portugal.

Bina later told me that this was her favorite stretch of the whole Camino, a section where she felt God's presence the most.

"I have always found the seaside to be a place for me to center myself," she said. "And walking along this section just reinforced all the reasons I wanted to walk this Camino."

Just short of Vila Praia de Âncora, we stopped for a late lunch at the Restaurante Camarão, which is perched on a hillside overlooking the Rio Âncora estuary. From our table on the veranda, we could see Vila Praia sprawled across the banks on the other side. Since the grilled codfish we ordered proved disappointingly dry, we figured we must have been paying for the view.

Afterward, we walked inland a short distance to reach the bridge that carries the N13 highway over the river into town, reaching our hotel, the Albergaria Quim Barreirer, around 4. We were delighted to find our two roller bags waiting for us, courtesy of Tuitrans, confirming that the luggage transfer process had worked, at least on this first day.

Not counting the hour for lunch, we had spent six hours walking 22 km. While it had been a full day, we still had plenty of time to relax and go out later to a nearby restaurant for dinner.

To finish the evening, we walked around Vila Praia's main square, where we found the church and fountain outlined in light, blue for the church and purple for the fountain. We bought some ice cream cones and enjoyed watching the people stroll around, the typical nighttime scene in a European city.

We returned to our hotel well satisfied with the first day of our "real Camino."

12

THE RIGHT KIND OF TORTILLAS

The next morning, we were up by 7, had breakfast at a nearby cafe and then walked to the church in the main square of Vila Praia de Âncora to resume our Camino. The temperature starting off was 72 degrees, promising to reach the mid-80s by the afternoon. It turned out to be another cloudless, sunny day from beginning to end.

North of Vila Praia, we passed some quiet stretches of beach unspoiled by development but we couldn't linger much to enjoy the views. Our mission for the morning was to catch a ferry across the Minho River at the border town of Caminha. This ferry crosses the river into Spain several times a day, but that schedule varies with the tide. We had been monitoring that schedule closely. On this day, we knew that we needed to catch the 11 a.m. boat across in order to reach our hotel in the Spanish town of A Guarda by late afternoon.

We entered Caminha on the main coastal road, which parallels the railroad tracks. In the city center, we stopped at the tourist information office just off the main square to get stamps for our credentials book. We had to ask the woman behind the counter to hurry because it was now only 10 minutes to 11.

Practically sprinting to the ferry landing, we bought our tickets and got the lady in the booth to stamp our second *sello* for the day as well. We then took seats on the car ferry's passenger deck. From there, we finally had a chance to admire Caminha's 19th century architecture — white buildings under pink terracotta tile roofs — just as we were pulling away from the dock.

A short distance into the channel, the ferry turned around to point toward the Spanish shore, which featured only a few scattered buildings. We settled back to enjoy the ocean breeze and the cries of gulls as they dipped and dived around the boat.

Disembarking 20 minutes later, we encountered no border controls or passport checks whatsoever. That's been the case ever since the formation of the European Union's Schengen Visa zone, in 1995. For tourists, crossing between EU countries is like passing from one U.S. state to another.

Now, we faced a choice of two routes into A Guarda: short or long. The short way is two kilometers long and follows a paved road, the Camino del Palomar, that reaches A Guarda after climbing a fairly steep hill. The long way consists of a mostly dirt path, six kilometers long, that meanders around the Santa Tegra Peninsula that extends into the Atlantic west of the ferry landing.

We opted for the long route, both to avoid the climb on the short route and to enjoy the woods and beach. Since it was only 11:30, we had plenty of time to reach A Guarda, so, let's saunter.

After a snack at the cafe near the Spanish ferry landing, we set off. The initial stretch, up to the point where the river empties into the Atlantic, took us past beaches crowded with Spanish sunbathers. It also led us into some difficult ground when the dirt path transitioned into soft sand.

That problem ended when we made the turn at the peninsula tip and headed north, a sweeping ocean vista to our left. Here, the beach consisted mostly of rocky outcroppings, whose beige color contrasted sharply with the deep blue of the sea. We soon reached a boardwalk, which we followed for most of the way into

A Guarda, whose buildings are arrayed in terraces up the hillside that overlooks its harbor.

Unlike Portuguese seaside towns, which feature white and terracotta as the predominant colors, the houses of A Guarda displayed a fuller palette, with blues, reds and grays mixing with the white and orange.

The day's walk, from Vila Praia de Ancora to the Hotel Celta in A Guarda, had covered nearly 21 km, so we had worked up a good appetite. On the advice of desk clerk Alexander, a personable young man who spoke five languages, we had dinner at the Puerto Guardes restaurant fronting the harbor, which turned out to be an excellent choice.

I had steak with mushroom sauce, a perfect comfort food for me. Bina enjoyed prawns and mussels, taking advantage of A Guarda's reputation for good seafood. Since we were planning to take the following day off, we also had a little alcohol with our meal, Bina trying out a regional wine (Albarino) and me a regional beer (Estrella Galicia).

We were in bed by 10 but didn't rouse ourselves until 9:30 the next morning. Then, we faced the problem of finding a nutritious breakfast, always a challenge in Spain.

The problem is that the Spanish (and Portuguese too) eat a late dinner, typically after 8:30 p.m., and don't require much in the morning except a coffee and pastry. That's about all that you can usually find at your typical cafe, which rarely operates a full kitchen in the morning.

As a diabetic, however, Bina needs to start the day with some protein, preferably eggs. The Hotel Celta's breakfast offering did not include any eggs, although Alexander said he would arrange for four hard boiled eggs to be provided for us the following morning. But for now, the only thing we could do was walk around town and see if we could find someone serving omelettes.

"I do not know of anybody in this neighborhood who does so," Alexander warned us.

It took us more than half an hour of wandering around, and a couple of inquiries in cafes that did not serve eggs, before we found one that offered *tortillas*, the Spanish word for omelettes. Not up to speed on the various types of *tortilla*, we first ordered a *Tortilla Espagnol*, which turned out to be cooked potato with some egg and cheese mixed in — too many carbs for Bina.

So, I ate that while she ordered a *Tortilla Francesca*, which a quick Google search on the iPhone had identified as a true egg omelette. Where would we be without Google? From this point on, we at least knew what kind of *tortilla* to look for on a Spanish breakfast menu. The fundamental problem remained, however: actually finding places that offered them.

The next morning, as Alexander had promised, the hotel kitchen prepared hard boiled eggs for us to eat with our bread and coffee. Reasonably fortified, we left the Hotel Celta at 9:15 a.m. and walked along foggy, misty streets with temperatures in the low 60s. This was the coolest morning we had encountered since leaving Porto on August 6 so we donned our Patagonia undershirts and rain jackets. As we headed up the coast, we could hear the waves crashing on the rocks but not actually see the shoreline, only the sea birds darting in and out of the fog.

Our Camino route from A Guarda mostly had us walking on the coastal highway, the PO-552, and a paved bicycle path to the side of that road. While the traffic was light, we found this highway walking to be rather monotonous compared to the pedestrian boardwalks we had enjoyed along the Portuguese coast. And the mist and fog continued to obscure the coastline views off to our left.

Just north of A Guarda, we did briefly deviate from the highway to pass through a kind of Galician rain forest of eucalyptus and pine trees, the tropical-like ferns dripping with moisture. Bina discovered that she is allergic to the smell of eucalyptus, which gives her a case of the sniffles.

Into the Galician rain forest ...

Eucalyptus? In Spain? Originating from Australia and south-east Asia, eucalyptus was planted on the Iberian Peninsula during the 19th century as a re-forestation project. The aromatic gum tree has the virtue of growing very quickly. But it also burns easily, because of the eucalyptus oil. The trees have been known to explode during fires. Walking through these forested areas, we noticed extensive swaths of blackened tree trunks, evidence of the forest fires that had raged through this region the previous year.

This is a perennial problem for northern Portugal and Spanish Galicia in the summer, when rainfall is limited. In some places, governments are cutting down the eucalyptus forests and planting indigenous trees to help control the fires.

Back along the highway, we encountered mostly open terrain fronting the ocean. An odd feature of this stretch was the occasional boat superstructure sticking up from the earth, as if somebody had sliced off the deck and thrown away the hull. We wondered if anybody actually lived in these structures or if they had simply been placed there as decoration. One way or the other, they make impressive lawn ornaments.

Nautical lawn ornaments?

We also saw an abundance of granaries, stone structures sitting on piers, formerly used to keep grain dry and safe from rodents. All through Spanish Galicia, people have restored these structures, known as hórreos, and kept them in their yards, apparently to preserve a sense of regional identity.

For Galicians, hórreos are us.

We stopped at a cafe in the old fishing village of Oia, which is known for its traditional stone houses and the monastery of Santa María la Real, a Romanesque structure from the 12th century that received an imposing Baroque façade in the 18th century. The table where we sat gave us a good view of the monastery.

While sipping our coffee, we chatted with a German couple seated at the table next to us. They had been following the same route as us from Porto and complained about their difficulties in finding accommodations. The woman, whose English was stronger than her husband's, did most of the talking.

"We used to like the flexibility of walking as long as we wanted each day and then stopping when we wanted to," she said. "But on this trip, we found it harder to do that since so many hotels and *albergues* turn out to be full, sometimes early in the afternoon. We feel we have to book ahead now. There are just too many people on this coast in August."

She was talking about those darn beachgoers, of course. In August, in Europe, the good weather comes at a cost.

Viladesuso, our destination for the evening, turned out to be a mostly modern town, completely lacking the ambience of Oia.

The Hotel Costa Verde, however, did provide us with the nicest room we had had so far on the Camino, spacious and comfortable, with enough room on the balcony to accommodate two chairs for watching the sun set over the Atlantic.

For dinner, Bina had arranged to meet a Facebook friend of hers, an American woman named Tanya Valdes, at the Porto dos Barcas restaurant in Viladesuso.

Tanya had walked the Camino several times and now wanted to open her own *albergue* on the trail. She had identified two potential locations: Oia, which we had visited earlier in the day, and a village near Caminha, in Portugal. She was finding it a great challenge, in both countries, to navigate the legal and real estate systems and negotiate with property owners.

"I consult several 'experts' but they tell me different things," Tanya said. "And the paperwork takes forever. You spend your time going from office to office to get signatures. Everything requires a stamp or signature."

Given these obstacles, Tanya's determination to "give back" was admirable. Here you had an American single woman from the Midwest eager to make a substantial investment from her life savings into a facility that would assist other *peregrinos*. And she wasn't alone. We had read about other pilgrims from outside the Iberian peninsula who had returned to operate *albergues* or cafes on the various Camino routes.[1]

For such people, the Camino de Santiago is so much more than just a walking trail. The physical trail, and the people who walk it, represent to them an ideal, an aspiration, whether that feeling is rooted in religious sensibility or something else. It's a form of love, actually.

---

1. By the time of this writing, Tanya had decided to locate her *albergue,* the La Cala Inn, in Oia. She is hoping to have it open by the summer of 2020.

13

PARADOR, BUT NO PARADISE

The next day differed dramatically from the previous one, weather-wise. Instead of haze and fog, we enjoyed clear skies, bright sunshine and blue ocean all the way north to Baiona, nearly 18 km up the coast. And to top it off, the sea breeze helped keep the temperatures down to the mid-70s.

As usual, we had two routes to choose from, one that hugged the coastline, the *Senda Litoral*, and another that veered slightly inland to approach Baiona over a range of hills. In our typical fashion, we opted to stay on the coastal path to enjoy the ocean view and avoid any climbing.

This may have been a mistake because the coastal route mostly took us along a busy highway, not our preferred walking path. The inland approach would have offered some sweeping vistas from the hills and gotten us into Baiona an hour or so earlier. This being our second day of consecutive walking, following our one-day break in A Guarda, we were feeling the strain in our legs a bit more today.

Our coastal walk did afford us a panoramic view of Baiona harbor when we rounded the point at Cabo Silleiro (Cape Silleiro). Straight ahead of us were the Polveiras and Carral islands and to the right was the bay that shelters the Baiona marina.

Behind us, on top of the mountain overlooking the cape, I spied what I thought were surely concrete gun emplacements, of the type you see on Normandy beach. These turned out to be fortifications built during the Spanish Civil War and maintained by the Spanish army until the late 1970s.

It was about 3 p.m. when we reached our hotel for the night, the Baiona Parador. These Paradors are former palaces, castles and monasteries taken over by the Spanish government and converted into luxury hotels. The Baiona Parador is not itself a historic building but rather a modern structure built in the style of a medieval Galician manor. It is, however, situated within the grounds of the medieval fortress protecting the city's harbor, so the entire property does have a historic feel to it.

Staying in this Parador represented a wild deviation from our typical Camino budget, but we had decided to stay here for one of our two nights in Baiona to "pamper" ourselves and get a good rest before continuing on to the major seaport of Vigo.

We immediately felt out of place when we entered the hotel grounds, being hot and sweaty after five hours of walking. "You must be tired," the bellman commented helpfully, as he carried our luggage upstairs. "Si, senor," I sighed. In fact, we both had naps as soon as he left the room.

We had hoped for an ocean view room, but instead we got one overlooking an interior courtyard. Okay, we thought, at least the room itself was quite spacious and comfortable. At 8:30 p.m., after showers and a change into more presentable clothes, we headed downstairs for a much-anticipated dinner. The meal was okay — Iberian ham for me, baked cod for Bina — but over-priced, in our opinion.

"It's tourist food," Bina commented.

Returning to the room around 10, we noticed that the interior courtyard below our window was now filled with people enjoying a noisy, catered party. They were still at it an hour later and the noise bubbled up to our third floor room, even with all the windows shut.

Uh oh. I went downstairs to complain — you're supposed to be able to get some sleep in a luxury hotel, right? The man behind the front desk said he couldn't do anything until midnight, when the party was scheduled to end. And the hotel being full, he couldn't move us to another room.

"This is Spain," he said, as if no other explanation was required.

By 12:15, the noise had abated only slightly, still preventing us from getting any sleep. Bina got on the phone and complained again. The clerk agreed to reduce our room rate by half. Yet, looking at our bill in the morning, we saw only a 30% reduction. More complaining from us attracted the attention of the manager, who grudgingly signed off on the 50%.

We left that morning thoroughly disgusted by our Parador experience. Despite the discount, we had still paid the highest rate of our Camino for the worst night's rest. Rather than Old World style and luxury, we had experienced something more akin to Las Vegas mass tourism.

For our second night in Baiona, we had picked the Hotel Rompeolas, which is located by the waterfront as you approach Baiona from the south. We had to take two single rooms, because they lacked a double, but were delighted to find that each room featured a balcony that overlooked the bay.

Once installed in the Rompeolas, we spent the rest of the afternoon and evening walking around Baiona, which is a popular tourist destination on the Spanish coast. At the Parque da Palma, which is located between the old town and the small peninsula upon which the Parador hotel sits, we found an array of parked food trucks offering cuisine from around the world. We could have had Texas barbecue, but instead chose German sausage and sauerkraut.

We both slept well that night, a huge difference from the Parador. Since we had a short day of walking planned, we took our time getting going that morning. Following a good breakfast at the hotel — with eggs! — we set off down the Baiona waterfront at 10:45 a.m. with the temperature in the low 60s. The walk took us past the Baiona marina, crowded with pleasure craft and a replica of Christopher Columbus' ship, the Pinta.

This painstaking recreation of a Spanish caravel had been moored in the harbor as a permanent exhibit to commemorate Baiona's chief claim to historical fame. On March 1, 1493, the Pinta became the first of Columbus' three vessels to report his discovery of the New World (remember from grade school: the Niña, Pinta and Santa Maria?). The Pinta arrived in Baiona harbor three days before Columbus himself sailed into Lisbon on the Niña.

Since we passed by the ship just before its opening time, 11 a.m., we were among the first visitors of the day and got a chance to explore it without having to jostle a lot of other tourists. That was fortunate because the caravel is a surprisingly small vessel, not offering a lot of comfort to a crew endeavoring to cross the Atlantic.

The exhibits inside the ship's hold described the hardships the crew had to contend with, such as the "nauseating" smell of the bilge water due to all the rotten things swirling around in the hold. Counter-intuitively, an inscription related, this smell actually "made the sailors feel peaceful" because it meant the caravel was not taking on *too much* water. We also learned of the discoveries Columbus' men brought back to Europe, such as corn, tobacco, parrots, iguanas, and a native invention that sailors have used ever since — hammocks.

Leaving Baiona behind, we continued up the coast to our next lodging, the El Retiro Hotel in Nigrán, only nine kilometers away. We had kept this walk short because it is nearly 30 km from Baiona to Vigo, the Spanish seaport where the Coastal

Portuguese Camino turns inland to meet the interior route at Redondela.

Knowing that 25 km represented, for us, the outer limit of a comfortable walk, I had tried to find a lodging place midway between Baiona and Vigo. Nigrán was the best I could do, which left us 20 km to do the next day.

At Nigrán, we encountered the Playa America, one of the largest and most popular beaches in northern Spain, over 1000 meters long and 30 meters wide. This being a Sunday in August, and a nice, sunny Sunday at that, the place was absolutely packed with sprawling sunbathers. In spots where the boardwalk petered out, Bina and I had to step around the half-naked bodies, feeling very much out of place in our heavy walking shoes and backpacks.

Outdoor market on Nigrán beach.

Checking into the El Retiro Hotel around 2 p.m., we had some lunch at the hotel restaurant and then took a nap. Waking two hours later, we decided that we still had some energy for additional walking. We were also eager to reduce the distance into Vigo the next day. From everything we had read in *peregrino* forums and blogs, walking through the southern industrial suburbs of Vigo would not be fun.

Studying the *Wisely* app, I identified a small beach just five kilometers north of us called Playa Portirão. If we cabbed up to that spot and then walked back to the hotel from there, we could eliminate five kilometers from the next day's walk to Vigo.

Getting to Playa Portirão by cab proved easy but walking back to the hotel was a little more difficult, as we found ourselves navigating a tangle of streets crowded with tourists on holiday. The late afternoon heat, in the low 80s, sapped our energy. Trying to follow the *Wisely* app, we encountered a few places where the Camino route simply petered out into stretches of beach, which had us picking our way around sunbathers again.

"I'm tired of all this this beach walking," Bina harrumphed, and I could only agree.

Dinner at the El Retiro's restaurant didn't help improve our mood much. Since we had to walk the next day, neither of us ordered wine with dinner, which puzzled the waiter.

"*No vino, no buen Camino!*" (No wine, no good walk), he said.

14

HUNTING SELLOS IN VIGO

Portirão Beach, where our taxi driver dropped us off, still lingered in the half light of dawn, as the rising sun in the east lit the offshore islands to the west in a pinkish glow. The beach itself, and the bobbing fishing boats anchored in the rock-protected bay, remained in semi-darkness. Four or five people slumbered in their sleeping bags near the sea wall as we walked by, having yet no reason to rouse themselves.

The odd thing was, this was 8:15 in the morning, well past sunrise in most countries. Bina and I had already breakfasted at the El Retiro Hotel in Nigran and taken a 10-minute taxi ride to this spot. And only now were we beginning to see daylight.

This is a peculiarity of the Spanish time zone, which is positioned in Central European Time (CET). That's *central*, as utilized by countries such as Poland and Germany, much further east of Spain. If you were to look at a time zone map, you would see that Spain — on the far western side of Europe — actually lines up time-wise with the U.K. and neighboring Portugal, which observe Greenwich Mean Time (GMT). As a result, for most of the year, the sun rises about an hour later in Spain than it "should," by the standards of most visitors. This being August, the difference was actually two hours, since Spain also follows Central European summer time.

In the U.K. or Portugal, our 8:15 a.m. view of Portirão Beach would have occurred at 6:15. The credit (or dis-credit) for this anomaly goes to Spain's former dictator, Francisco Franco. Nazi Germany had provided critical assistance to Franco during the Spanish Civil War (1936-39) that brought him to power. Hitler asked him to return that favor after Germany launched World War II.

Having little else to offer — Spain was in ruins after 1939 — Franco moved Spain from GMT to CET in 1940 as a sign of solidarity. And there it has remained ever since, a constant nuisance to foreign visitors.

The temperature was still a cool 63 degrees as we began our walk to Vigo, although the clear skies promised more heat later in the day. The initial part turned out to be relatively pleasant, as we wound our way through one coastal suburb after another, occasionally finding ourselves on a hill offering a view of the ocean. As expected, however, the scenery became more industrial and commercial as we got closer to Vigo.

One startling exception to that rule was the nude beaches. These were small areas, typically isolated by rocks, in which you would see mostly paunchy middle-aged males hanging around soaking up the sun. The few women about went topless rather than full *au natural*, except for one younger woman laid out on the grass in a park-like spot above the beach. For the sake of pedestrians, Bina and I agreed, nude beaches should enforce age limits!

By the time we reached the harbor area of Vigo, about 12:45 p.m., we had covered 15 km since Portirão Beach and decided to call it a day. We were just standing there, on a busy street corner, asking ourselves: do we really want to slog a couple more kilometers through this traffic and up those steep hills to get to our hotel? No? Well, okay, I feel the same way.

We cabbed it to the Oca Ipanema Hotel, which is located in a relatively upscale, trendy part of the city, just a few blocks from a shopping mall. The nearby streets hosted several good restaurants. All in all, a good place to hang out for two days.

What Vigo lacks in charm and ambience, it does offer a commercial dynamism rare in the rest of Galicia. The city's origins date back to Roman times but it experienced its most rapid growth in the 19th and 20th centuries, fueled by the marine and automotive industries. Vigo is the largest fishing port in Europe and a Peugeot car assembly plant constitutes its leading employer.

Our first task was to wash two days' worth of clothes in the sink and hang them up to dry in the room. Then, we took a 20 minute walk back down to the harbor area to get our *sellos* for the day. We found two tourism offices, right across the street from each other. One was operated by the city government and the other by the regional authorities of Galicia. This proved very convenient for us because Vigo marked the beginning of the first 100 km to Santiago. From this point on, we needed two stamps each day, not just one.

The next day, our down day in Vigo, we decided to get some church stamps, which always look better in a credentials book than those from cafes or restaurants. Following the advice an employee in the Galician office had give us the previous day, we decided to try two churches: Maria Auxliadora and Santiago de Vigo. We found the doors to the Auxliadora church open when we arrived. We wandered inside, only to find nobody there.[1]

Churches, at least in Portugal, often maintain a table or counter where they leave the wooden stamp and ink pad for a *sello* but not this one. So, we decided to proceed to the Santiago de Viga church, which Google Maps said was only eight minutes away.

On the way, we passed the Peregrinus Cafe. Ah, I thought, surely a "Pilgrim's Cafe" would offer *sellos*. They did, but the staff of this particular establishment were rude and surly this morning. The waiter took forever to take our order for coffee and seemed irritated when we followed up with a request for stamps. He handed our credentials to a woman behind the counter, who was more interested in tidying up the bar than stamping our booklets.

Bina finally walked up to her to see if she could push things along. With a dismissive gesture, the woman stamped the wrong boxes in our credentials books and even put Bina's stamp wrong side up. It was the worst experience we had had so far getting a *sello*.

And we still needed one more to meet the two-per-day requirement. We walked on to the Santiago de Vigo church feeling not very optimistic. Again, we found no stamp table inside. All we could see were a few people praying in the pews and a priest talking to a man in the confessional box. Then, Bina noticed a young *peregrino* couple leaving the church. I quickly intercepted them to ask them if they had been able to obtain a *sello*. The man said that a priest behind the pulpit had given them one.

By this time, Bina was chatting with the custodian, a kindly old man who escorted her to the rear of the church, where a young priest wearing glasses asked if we were *peregrinos*. Receiving our affirmative reply, he took our credentials books with him into a back office and stamped them, handing them back with a smile. We thanked him effusively.

This turned out to be our typical experience in Spanish churches. In the matter of obtaining *sellos,* you need to find a priest to ask, rather than look for the self-service option that is often provided in Portuguese churches.

---

1. In a side chapel, we did encounter an odd statute of a saint in a modern business suit, something we had never seen before in a Catholic church.

You typically see saints in Roman, Medieval or Renaissance style clothing, since most of them come from those earlier periods. A reader of Bina's blog on our trip later suggested that this was Saint Dominic Savio, an Italian boy who died at age 14 and was canonized in 1954 for living his short life in purity.

15

THE CAMINO PROVIDES

W e woke up the next day, at 7:30, to a foggy morning. It was still cloudy by the time we finished breakfast at the hotel and the temperature a cool 62, good walking weather. The desk called us a taxi, which deposited us at the Pulperia A Nosa Rúa on the outskirts of Vigo.[1]

The taxi driver who picked us up at the hotel seemed a little surprised at our destination, describing the Pulperia A Nosa Rúa as a *"nada lugar"* (nothing place). Indeed, we disembarked in front of a shuttered up, sidewalk-fronting restaurant/bar in a nondescript working class district. But I had chosen this place on purpose, because it was located on the Camino just within the city limits.

Once we resumed our walk at 9:20 a.m., we quickly left urban Vigo behind and entered the forested park areas of the Monte da Madroa, location of the Vigo Zoo. From here we climbed some hills that afforded us panoramic views of the Vigo estuary and its mussel traps, which are barge-like structures anchored in rows in the river. To the right, we could see the Ponte de Rande, a highway bridge that crosses the Vigo River to connect Vigo with Pontevedra to the north. Even the commercial sprawl of Vigo itself, to the left, appeared quite scenic from this distance.

From there, we began heading in a northeasterly direction, away from the coast and deeper into the forest of ferns, pine and eucalyptus trees, the standard foliage in this part of the Iberian peninsula. Halfway to Redondela, we encountered a delightful cafe known as O Eido Vello. Perched on a little summit overlooking the trail, it featured a veranda with tables and chairs that afforded views of the surrounding forest and the Vigo River.

After the owner had brought our coffee to the veranda, we asked her a question that had been puzzling us for several days: why do Spanish restaurants rarely serve vegetables? Typically, the only greens you get come in a salad.

"I'm not really sure," the young woman said, "but I think it's because the Spanish people are really set in their ways. They have this idea in their heads about what a restaurant is supposed to serve. They eat plenty of vegetables in their own houses, so that's not the issue. But when they go to a restaurant, they like to eat nicer things that they don't usually get at home."

Resuming our walk, we started noticing vandalism on the official trail markers. These are stone steles that incorporate three elements: the Camino logo of stylized yellow scallop shell on a blue background, a yellow arrow pointing in the direction of travel, and a small metal strip with the number of kilometers left to Santiago de Compostela. On every stele that we passed in that area, someone had removed the kilometer readings from the stone.

At first, we surmised that this was just because the authorities had not yet gotten around to figuring out the distances for each monument. Later, we read blog commentary indicating that this was actually vandalism and could be found in other parts of the Camino as well. I couldn't begin to think why thieves would want to deface these markers except to express some personal spite.

Walking along the mountain tops between Vigo and

Redondela did not prove very taxing. But the sharp descent into Redondela did exert stress on Bina's knees and ankles. She had to walk down the road in a Z pattern, a tactic I employed as well.

Once we had reached level ground, we stopped by a municipal fountain and had our snack. We noticed several locals driving up to fill plastic canisters from the fountain, a common practice in towns around here. Most of the houses do have access to piped-in municipal water, which is fine for bathing and dish washing purposes. But for drinking water, people prefer these old fountains that provide water from natural springs.

Redondela is a mid-size Spanish town where the two routes of the *Camino Portugués* combine — the interior route that crosses the Spanish frontier at Valença and the coastal path from Caminha that Bina and I had been walking. The two routes come together at a traffic junction near the center of town.

Standing there for a short time, it's easy to see that the majority of pilgrims arrive via the interior route. Up until this moment, Bina and I had seen only a smattering of fellow *peregrinos* during our coastal stroll. Now, for the next 85 km, from Redondela to Santiago de Compostela, we were to see a lot more.

Redondela's other claim to fame, two 19th century railroad viaducts that dominate the skyline coming into town, also merit a quick look. But otherwise, Bina and I were eager to keep on going, since we still had seven kilometers to cover before reaching our lodging in Arcade.

Actually getting out of Redondela proved a little troublesome because the middle of town is characterized by narrow lanes that intersect at odd angles. We would be walking along, eyes glued to our Wisely app, and suddenly realize that the cursor designating our location was off the Camino. So, back we went to the last intersection to try again. The official yellow route arrows weren't plentiful enough in this tangle to be of much help. Twice, we had to inquire of locals for the correct way.

Bina, by now, was experiencing some other difficulties. "I just don't feel right. I feel like I'm walking in a fog," she commented, as we headed out of Redondela.

We stopped to rest on a bus stop bench. For the first time in the trip, she pulled out the blood tester kit she carried in her backpack. This device has a needle that she uses to prick a finger to extract a tiny sliver of blood, which she squeezes onto a test strip that she inserts into a small hand-held meter. The reading showed 89, low for her. A more normal reading would be in the 110 range.

The only solution was to get some carbs into her system, to raise her count. By eating some crackers that she carried in her pack, she stabilized a little, but still needed more carbs, preferably some sort of sugared drink.

We walked on, hoping to run into a small cafe. But the road leading out of Redondela took us into a residential suburb without any such facility in sight. Starting to get worried, we discussed backtracking into Redondela, which could rob an hour from our schedule. We didn't relish doing that because it was already mid-afternoon and reaching Arcade would take us at least another hour and a half.

Then, while passing a farming supply company, I noticed the oddest thing: a recessed cinderblock wall housing a vending machine! Was this a mirage? Peering more closely, I could see a lit up exterior testifying that this machine was indeed plugged in and functioning. Not only that, but the products included the kind of sugared fruit drink that Bina needed at this point.

"The Camino provides" is a saying often heard among *peregrinos*, meaning that whatever trouble or difficulty you get into on the trail, some solution will materialize. For the first time, we experienced the truth of that axiom.

The drink helped restore Bina's glucose count to 134, which was what she needed to get through the rest of the day. And that was important because we we still had some hard walking to finish up, most of it on paved roads that crossed rolling farmland in full sun and 80 degree temperatures.

The last stretch, outside Arcade, proved particularly harrowing as it involved walking alongside a major highway while trucks thundered past. It wasn't until 4:45 p.m. when we finally reached the Hotel Restaurante Isepe in Arcade, somewhat the worse for wear after walking 22 km that day.

We took some consolation, however, from the fact that the next day's stretch, from Arcade to Pontevedra, would be only 13 km. After that, we could enjoy a planned down day in Pontevedra.

---

1. In Central America, *pulperia* denotes a small general store. In Spain, however, the word refers to a restaurant or bar that serves octopus.

16

MEDIEVAL TIMES

Leaving our hotel in Aracade at 9:30 a.m., we immediately experienced the full effect of the merging of the two Portuguese routes. When we first stepped into the streets to follow the path out of town, we heard behind us the clicking of trekking poles on the cobblestones. It was two young men, who passed us just before we reached the Puente Sampaio bridge.

After crossing the Verdugo River on this medieval, stone-arched bridge, we looked back to see clumps of other *peregrinos* in motion behind us. I counted at least 10. Within five minutes, I was counting up to 20 other trekkers, both ahead and behind.

"The trickle has become a torrent," I said to Bina.

About an hour out of Arcade, we stopped at a trailside cafe for a coffee and Coke Zero and chatted with the proprietor in our basic Spanish. He estimated that about 300 pilgrims passed by each day in August. We just shook our heads, imagining what it must be like on the last 100 km of the Camino Frances, where you could expect to see thousands in a day.

Sitting there at the cafe, we also learned a little bit about trail etiquette. A young couple walked up and asked about a *baño* (restroom). The cafe did feature an outside facility, with one door labelled *"senõrs"* and the other *"senõras,"* but the doors were locked, as the couple found out when they tried to open them.

"*Sin aqua,* (no water)," the owner's wife told them. "*Roto* (broke)." The couple returned to the trail with disappointed looks.

Bina, who had been sitting next to the woman during this exchange, figured it out at once. She had noticed other people using the *baño* previously. She had also observed that the young couple had not purchased a coffee or snack.

"They didn't buy anything, did they?" she asked.

The woman shook her head dismissively. "No, they just wanted to use the bathroom. If we let them do that, everyone on the trail will be coming over here to use the bathroom and we'll have a mess."

Finding a place to relieve oneself is indeed a constant problem on the Camino. Public facilities are rare in cities and towns, so you end up stopping at a cafe, whether you really want a coffee or not. On the trail itself, the only solution is to go behind a tree and ask your partner to watch for other hikers coming around the bend. Nine times out of ten, when you do find a convenient place to squat down, you will encounter physical evidence that many *peregrinos* before you had identified the same spot for this purpose.

Camino veterans say the problem of unsightly toilet trash gets worse every year. On some parts of the trail, volunteer groups have banded together to conduct periodic cleanup campaigns. But these efforts are clearly insufficient to keep up with the increasing number of *peregrinos* on the Camino

Leaving the cafe, we continued to to Pontevedra, mostly through woodland with the usual pines, eucalyptus and ferns. By 1 p.m., we reached the outskirts of Pontevedra, where our hotel was located. It being too early to check in, we relaxed at the cafe next door and watched the constant parade of *peregrinos* straggling into town.

Pontevedra is the second largest town in Galicia, after Santiago de Compostela, and features an abundance of accommodations. But August is high season and we noticed people being turned away from the *albergue* located just across the street from where we were sitting. We were glad we had arrived in Pontevedra with a reservation.

Our hotel, the Peregrino Hostal, opened its doors at 2, enabling us to check in. After a brief nap, we washed some clothes in the sink and Bina spoke to our daughter in Atlanta via Skype. Then, we walked on into the center of town to visit the tourist office to obtain our *sellos* and find some place to eat dinner.

Our plan at this point was to spend the next day, Friday, relaxing in Pontevedra, before setting out for our next destination, Caldas de Reis, on Saturday. Since Caldas was over 24 km from Pontevedra, we planned to do a partial walk in that direction on Friday to reduce the following day's distance. We sought advice from the tourism office about where we might walk to in order to conveniently cab it back to Pontevedra. The best bet seemed to be a church in a small town called Alba.

On the recommendation of the woman in the tourist office, we then had dinner at the nearby Hotel Ruas, which is located on one of the squares in Pontevedra's medieval quarter. It was good comfort food. Bina ordered fish and I pork chops. We both enjoyed a helping of vegetables, which is not common on Spanish dinner menus. We got back to the Peregrino Hostal about 9:45, looking forward to a good night's sleep.

Unfortunately, Bina was troubled by a smell in the room, probably caused by cleaning disinfectant, which irritated her asthma. She is intensely allergic to mold, mildew, cat dander and certain other chemical smells. She had noticed an odor when we first checked in, but figured the smell would go away over time.

But the smell had remained and she spent a troubled night. We tried opening the windows but this introduced some street noise.

At some point in the wee hours, we decided that we had had enough. For our second night in Pontevdra, we needed to stay in a place with air conditioning, which could overcome smells such as this. I did a quick search on booking.com and noticed that the Hotel Ruas, where we had enjoyed a good dinner, did have air conditioning. So, I made the reservation.

The next morning, we didn't drag ourselves out of bed until 9:30. Even so, we proceed with our plan of knocking some distance off the following day's walk. After breakfast at the cafe next door, we asked the hotel to arrange for a cab to meet us at the Alba church at 1 p.m. Then, we set off from the hotel at 11:30 carrying very light packs, with just water and a few snacks.

We walked through Pontevedra, crossed the Ponte do Burgo bridge over the Lérez river and passed through some suburbs on the other bank before entering a charming landscape of woodlands and small towns. We covered nearly six kilometers on this walk, really pushing ourselves in the last half hour because we were worried about missing our taxi ride.

In fact, at 1:10 p.m., still a quarter kilometer before reaching the church, we encountered the taxi coming down the road towards us. The driver, obviously looking for his fare, already had the meter running. The ride back to the hotel cost us 13 euros, a bit more than we had originally calculated.

Upon reaching the hotel, we had lunch at the cafe next door and then packed for our shift to the Hotel Ruas. Taking a cab, we arrived at 4:30 p.m. and found that our room was located on the very top floor. Without the air conditioning, the room would have been very hot this time of year. At least there was no strong smell to aggravate Bina's asthma. Around 7, we went downstairs to have dinner.

As we had the previous evening, we sat at a table on the front patio of the hotel, which fronted one of the main squares of the old town. We noticed both children and adults wandering around in medieval costume, knowing that this evening marked the beginning of Pontevedra's Feira Franca (French Fair), a medieval festival that would last the weekend.

This event, which was launched by the city council of Pontevedra in the early 2000s, ostensibly is designed to commemorate the decision by King Henry IV of Castile to grant the city the right to hold a tax-free open market for one month, from the last two weeks of August to the first two weeks of September. Figuring that this would be like Viana do Castelo's *Nossa Senhora da Agonia* party all over again, Bina and I were glad to be hoofing out of town the next morning.

Except, that we weren't.

Bina's meal included a goat cheese salad and *croquetas* (fried cheese balls). We suspect that one of those options was a poor choice because she went to bed that night with an upset stomach. By the next morning, she was throwing up whatever was left in her stomach. She was in no shape to do anything but lie in bed. We decided that she would need at least another day to recover, so resuming the Camino the next day was out of the question.

I had to move fast to extend our stay at the Hotel Ruas by two days and then redo our accommodations for several succeeding days, which also meant rescheduling our luggage transfer arrangements. First the Hotel Ruas. The man at the front desk said a family was slated to take the room we were currently in for that night, but he could (thankfully!) offer us a smaller room down the hall. Done.

Next, I called Tuitrans, which was scheduled to pick up our luggage that very morning for transport to Caldas de Reis. Could they please, please cancel the morning's pickup and let me send them a revised schedule by day's end? Yes, they could.[1]

Then, it was a mater of getting on booking.com and cancelling and then rescheduling the next several days worth of bookings. With each cancellation, I pleaded Bina's sickness and asked them to refrain from imposing penalties on us because of the short time frame. All of them agreed.

It had been a frantic morning and our problems were, by no means over. But at least we had a room for the coming night in which Bina could recover. She was now running a low grade fever and slept through most of the day, leaving me to run errands, such as obtaining our Camino stamps for the day and picking up some lunch.

I obtained the first stamp at the Santuario de la Vergin Peregrina, an 18th century Baroque chapel built in the shape of a scallop shell. On the high altar perched a statue of the *Divina Peregrina* (Divine Pilgrim), the virgin saint who guided pilgrims to Santiago. This angelic figure with golden curls was outfitted as a traditional pilgrim. She wore a floppy hat and traveling purse at her belt, but in the most regal style imaginable, with a white gown and green robe embroidered in gold. She held a golden staff in her right hand and the baby Jesus cradled in her left. It seemed an appropriate place to pray for Bina's swift recovery from her food poisoning.

I asked the man at the entrance who provided the *sellos* where I could obtain my second stamp for the day and he suggested the city's main basilica, about 15 minutes away. I arrived there just after 11, as Mass was beginning. Fortunately, the elderly woman at the entrance table was gracious enough to provide me the second stamp.

Mission for the day accomplished, I went back to the hotel and found Bina still fast asleep. So, I went out again in search of lunch.

There were more options than usual today on the streets of Pontevedra. The *Feira Franca* was now in full swing and huge crowds of people dressed in medieval costumes milled about the streets browsing the various craft exhibits, children's rides and food booths. The tangy smell of grilling chicken hung thick in the summer air.

Musicians strolled through the streets playing traditional instruments and a long-tailed dragon came snaking through the streets, its mouth expelling bursts of actual fire. The men inside the costume had somehow contrived to install a flame thrower up there to delight the kids (and adults) with some fearsome pyrotechnics. Rotisseried bystander, anyone?

Also popular was a round cage in which condemned criminals were locked up — volunteers, only — and then hoisted several feet into the air by the bailiff and his helpers.

Incarceration has never been so much fun.

Leery of the street food because of what had happened to Bina, I opted for the simplest, most straightforward fare I could find: Burger King. Yes, Pontevedra sported a Burger King in the old quarter, albeit one that subtly blended in with the surrounding architecture. No tall pole with a Burger King logo and certainly no drive-in, since it fronted a pedestrian-only street.

I felt almost embarrassed standing in line with all the Spanish children and teenagers. But all I wanted after weeks of

Portuguese and Spanish food was a big sloppy burger with cheese and fries. So, I went for it. And I'm happy to relate that my stomach felt none the worse for the experience. In fact, I went back later that evening and had the same thing for dinner.

Except for eating some food that I brought her from the hotel restaurant, Bina stayed in bed the entire day and never saw any of the festival. We calculated later that she must have slept 30 hours after coming down with the food poisoning. Some of this sleeping may have been related to exhaustion, as the long days on the Camino finally caught up with her.

In any case, it was still going to be touch and go whether she could return to the trail the next day, Sunday.

---

1. Tuitrans' performance during our Camino was stellar. They always delivered our luggage to the right place and accommodated us when we had to make changes.

17

MUSICAL INTERLUDE

S aturday night proved a restless one for me. Even though we were three floors up, on the Hotel Rua's highest floor, the street noise was relentless, as people partied deep into the wee hours. When I went downstairs to check out the breakfast options in the morning, the restaurant was full of bleary-eyed men still in medieval garb — truly dedicated party animals trying to clear their heads with coffee.

Bina felt better this morning, to the point where she was able to keep down some boiled eggs and a toast. Reviewing the situation, she professed herself able to resume walking, but uncertain how far she could get.

This put us in a logistical bind. We were scheduled to stay one more night in Pontevedra. For the following Monday, we had booked a hotel in Padrón, a full 45 km to the north. The midway point between Pontevedra and Padrón is the thermal springs town of Caldas de Reis. If we could reach Caldas today, Sunday, we could easily cab it back to Pontevedra for the evening and then return to Caldas the next day to walk to Padrón by Monday evening, which would put us back on our proper Camino schedule.

Failing to reach Caldas today would leave us too much ground to cover on Monday and possibly require changing our bookings and luggage transport schedule again.

Thankfully, we had been able to knock six kilometers off the distance to Caldas with the walk to the Alba church on Friday. So, if we resumed today from that church, we faced just 19 km to Caldas, normally a doable saunter for us. Everything depended on how Bina held up during today. We stocked up on lots of packets of Propel (an electrolyte replacement drink) and set off.

The taxi dropped us off at the church at 10:15 and we began walking along some wooded paths paralleling the railroad tracks. Because of the late start, we encountered few other *peregrinos*, many of whom had likely left Pontevedra a good deal earlier than us. We enjoyed having the Camino mostly to ourselves, although heat became an issue as the temperature rose to 88 degrees by late afternoon. The trail included sections of open terrain, including corn fields and vineyards.

Bina's stomach remained a bit uncertain but her strength and confidence improved the farther we walked. I kept assuring her that we could stop anytime she wished. But she continued drinking lots of Propel and insisted that she could make it all the way to Caldas de Reis. I knew she was on the mend by the way she kept sampling grapes from the trellises we passed along the way.

"I'm testing the quality of the local wine," she quipped.

We got a moral boost near the end when we fell in with a personable Dutch fellow named William. Although younger and much more athletic than us, William slowed down to chat with us, which made the last hour go by faster.

About 30 minutes outside Caldas, the three of us entered a small village with a square and benches. A group of about 20 German women *peregrinas* were sitting around the square singing songs in their native language that sounded like hymns. We stood there entranced by the beauty of the voices and melodies.

"It was a true Camino moment," Bina said later. "The music stayed with me and carried me forward to Caldas."

We reached the town's main square at 4:30 and soon found a taxi to take us back to Pontevedra. The decision to push on to Caldas de Reis, although initially hard for Bina, paid off for us in that it made the next day's walk, from Caldas to Padron, manageable at 21 km.

We began that Monday, September 3, with our last breakfast at the Hotel Ruas in Pontevedre. We had spent a lot more time in this hotel than we had planned but the hotel staff had been considerate throughout the period of Bina's illness. Manuel, the young man working the morning shift, for the second morning in a row, got the kitchen staff to prepare a few boiled eggs for Bina, which was something not featured on their menu. I had a ham-and-cheese sandwich. Manual also arranged for our taxi ride to Caldas, where we arrived about 9:30 a.m.

Caldas de Reis has been famous since Roman times for its thermal springs, whose mineral water flows at a constant temperature of 104 degrees F. The Romans named the place Aquae Calidae (Hot Water) and ran one of their famous roads through it, traces of which can still be seen along the Camino path. Since the 19th century, it has been known for its spa hotels, which attract guests who like to bathe in the warm mineral waters, often for therapeutic purposes. Before Bina came down with food poisoning, we had actually booked ourselves into one of these hotels, the Balneario Acuña.

Testing out the thermal springs there would have been interesting. But on this day, Caldas de Reis represented only a place on the map to start our morning walk. And before doing that, we decided to find the tourist information office in order to pick up our first stamp of the day.

This proved to be more difficult than it should have been. The previous afternoon, we had noticed a sign for this office on the right side of the main highway entering Caldas. We asked the taxi driver to drop us off near that sign and then scouted out the buildings on that side of the road.

No sign of the tourism office, but we did find a public library and went inside to ask the librarian where that office might be. She took us next door to a shuttered-up building and pointed to a sign in the window announcing that the tourism office had moved. No mention, however, of where the office had moved.

After quizzing the librarian, in our basic Spanish, we understood her to say: cross back to the other side of the street and find a gray-painted building near the Froiz supermarket. So, back across the street we went. Checking Google Maps, we saw that Caldas contained two Froiz markets. Which one?

We asked one old gentleman sitting on a bench for directions to the tourism office. He helpfully pointed back across the street, toward the library. Obviously, he had not received the memo about the move.

Continuing to rely on the librarian's guidance, we followed Google Maps to the nearest of the Froiz stores, several blocks away. Several of the buildings on that street were kind of gray-ish — you know, basic cinder block — but one looked more gray-ish than the others. Approaching the glass doors, we saw no tourist information logo but we could see a young woman at the front desk with piles of brochures around her and boxes cluttering the floor.

Responding to our inquiry when we walked in, the woman did affirm that, yes indeed, this was the tourist office and she stamped our credentials books. Otherwise, she seemed more interested in looking at her computer monitor than in responding to our other questions about the Camino path and what kind of weather we could expect that day.

When we complained about the difficulty we had had locating her office, she gave us a so-what look and went back to her Web browsing. This was clearly an office that did not want to be found by actual customers.

We finally set off from Caldas at 10:15, a good bit later than our typical Camino start. It was a cloudy morning and still a bit cool at 70 degrees. Because of some fine mist, we initially donned our rain jackets but removed them as the skies cleared toward noon.

At one rest stop by a stream, we encountered the German women that we had met the previous day. Hoping that they might burst into song again, we sat down on a bench and had our snack as they milled about nearby.

The leader of the group soon asked them to bunch up in order for her to take a video. To our delighted surprise, they suddenly erupted in "Happy Birthday," in English! Somebody back home, apparently, was going to get a nice birthday greeting.

I've previously mentioned how public rest rooms are scarce on the Camino Portugués. There is an exception to that rule. As we got closer to Santiago, we began noticing a few that were located just off the trail and actually featured vending machines, for snacks, coffee and cold drinks, and a few tables and chairs, or benches. These are operated by the volunteer pilgrim associations that have sprung up in recent years to help maintain the trail. Marvelous places, with actual running water and toilet paper! We passed one outside Caldas de Reis and another, a few hours later, in Infesta, a suburb of Pontecesures.

While leaving the one at Infesta, we encountered a woman walking by herself. She gave her name as Corina and said she lived in Mexico City. Noting that her features were more European than Indian, we probed further and found that her parents came from Galicia. She had moved to Mexico when she was a young child. For her, therefore, this Camino was a kind of homecoming.

"I had always wanted to travel back here and see the land that my parents came from," Corina said. "Walking the Camino is the best way for me to see the country and experience the culture."

We split up with Corina on the outskirts of Padrón, where she was scheduled to meet with some friends at a nearby hotel. We continued walking north up the Sar River, through an industrial area, until we reached our lodging for the night. We arrived at the Hotel Chef Rivera, in the center of town, shortly before 4.

The timing proved fortuitous. Not having eaten anything except snacks since breakfast, Bina and I were anxious to get some kind of full meal at the hotel. Spanish restaurants typically offer lunch or dinner only at certain hours.

In this case, the hotel was about to close down its kitchen for lunch and would not open for dinner that evening because it was a Monday. Many Spanish (and Portuguese) restaurants close on both Sunday and Monday. Fortunately, the kitchen manager was kind enough to stay open just for us and we both went for a full lunch: *zamburiñas* (baked scallops) and a vegetable potpourri for Bina, steak and a Galician broth soup for me.

After a long five plus hours on the trail, this meal really hit the spot. And because we had lunch so late, there was no need to do more for dinner that night than finish off our snacks.

18

SOME ARE HOT, AND SOME ARE NOT

I t had been our plan to spend the next day, Tuesday, in Padrón and then resume our walk on Wednesday, September 5. On Tuesday morning, we noticed the Weather Channel reporting a strong chance of rain for Wednesday. Rain had always been our *bête noire* on the Camino, something we tried to avoid at all costs. That, combined with the fact that Bina was not yet 100% back to par, made us decide to rest for two days in Padrón rather than one.

We had to rush this decision because the Hotel Chef Rivera was filling up fast for Wednesday and we wanted to keep our room. I was able to make the necessary lodging changes on booking.com with no penalty and Tuitrans, our luggage service, adjusted their last two pickups for us as well.

We didn't begrudge the last walking day because we knew that hanging around Padrón could actually help prepare us, spiritually, for the completion of our pilgrimage. The city has played a central role in the post-Biblical traditions associated with St. James.

According to these stories, which first emerged in written form in the 9th century, the apostle James traveled from Palestine to Spain, sometime after Jesus' crucifixion, to spread the gospel in what was then a prosperous Roman province. His boat is purported to have landed at Iria Flavia, a port at the confluence of the Sar and Ulla rivers that later became Padrón.

After James suffered martyrdom in Palestine, the stories relate, his followers shipped his body back to Iberia by boat, which landed in Iria Flavia. From there, the remains were transferred further north to Santiago de Compostela, which is why the cathedral built in that city became the destination point for the Camino de Santiago pilgrimage.

As a non-Catholic, I don't feel obligated to take any personal stand on the authenticity of the St. James-in-Iberia traditions. Catholic scholars themselves have argued about the issue over the centuries. I do suggest, however, that anyone walking the Camino will find it useful, possibly inspirational, to soak up a bit of the ambience surrounding the story of St. James. After all, that's what originally got us all walking to Santiago in the first place. So, during the two days we spent in Padrón, Bina and I took the time to visit all the major sites associated with the Apostle.

To cover James' initial visit to Iberia, we went searching for Iria Flavia, the old Roman port. This is located on the northeastern outskirts of Padrón, just past where the N-550 highway crosses the Sar River. Sadly, no Roman ruins remain. All we could do was visit a church dedicated to St. Mary that was built on the site of the Roman settlement. By tradition, the Virgin Mary inspired James to venture to Iberia.

Originally constructed in the Gothic style in the 13th century, this church received a Baroque makeover in the 17th century. We arrived just as two ladies were preparing to close the doors for the afternoon. They graciously allowed us to peek inside and even obtain a *sello*.

The other site related to James' arrival in Iria Flavia is the Santiaguino do Monte shrine, situated at the top of Mount San Gregorio overlooking Padrón. From our hotel, we only had to walk a few minutes to the *Paseo de Espolón*, that park-like esplanade that runs parallel to the Sar River in the center of town.

At the main church, the Santiago de Padrón, we crossed the river on the medieval stone bridge, from which you have a clear view of the "Carmo" (Carmelite) monastery dominating the opposite bank. Guided by our *Wisely* app, we turned right at the fountain that sits at street level in front of the steps leading to the monastery. From there, it's a short distance to the 132 stone steps that ascend the hill to the shrine, skirting the monastery walls.

At the top, we found a collection of boulders surmounted by a stone cross marking the place where St. James is said to have preached. A fountain nearby commemorates a legend of him striking the stone with his staff to generate water for the faithful.

The area around the Santiaguino has been turned into a park, with picnic tables, where some young people practiced walking on a tightrope strung between two trees. The only other people we encountered was a couple taking photos of the shrine.

The last major "Jacobean" (Latin for "James") site in Padrón is the *pedron (Galician for "big stone")*, which is housed under the altar in the Santiago de Padrón church. When St. James' boat reached Iria Flavia from Palestine, the sailors — or angels, according to popular legend — guiding the vessel supposedly tied it up at this stone, then in use as a bollard.

Some Latin engraved on the stone indicates that it was originally dedicated to Neptune, the Roman sea god, and thus had served as a point of religious devotion for some time before James arrived in the area. Irregardless, viewing the *pedron* gets today's pilgrim as close as they're ever going to get — at least symbolically — to the origins of the Camino de Santiago story.

After musing over the stone for a few minutes — at the end of the day, it's just a rock — Bina and I sat down in the pews to pray and reflect. At one point, Bina walked back to the entrance, where a woman worked behind a desk providing *sello* stamps to *pere-*

grinos and information handouts to other tourists who wandered into the church.

Hearing some raised voices, I walked back to see what was going on. Bina was interpreting, in Spanish, for a middle-aged German woman, a *peregrina* with her backpack, who was trying to ask questions of the church lady. The German was thinking about walking to the Herbon Monastery, which is located about three kilometers out of town, and wanted to know if the monks might provide lunch when she arrived, since there are no restaurants in that area. The church lady advised her to get her own lunch in town before proceeding to the monastery.

I marveled at the German woman's pluck and dedication to completing her pilgrimage. Although gray-haired and frail, she had walked all the way from Porto to Padrón by herself.

Other than its association with St. James, Padrón has other claims to fame, such as Rosalía de Castro, Galicia's adored 19th century poetess. Although she was born in Santiago de Compostela (and is buried there), de Castro lived most of her life in Padrón, where the family house is maintained as a museum.

We visited the museum on our way to the Iria Flavia church and found a well preserved collection of documents and exhibits related to her life. It is difficult for outsiders to appreciate the importance of this woman to Galician culture. She wrote her poems in Gallego, the Galician language, rather than in Spanish, which endeared her to people who feel themselves culturally distinct from the rest of Spain. All over Padrón, you see old photographs of de Castro hanging in shops and restaurants, including the bar of our hotel. You can even buy a T-shirt with her image.

And then there's the Padrón Pepper, a green pepper that originates from this area but is now grown in many places around the world. You find it in *tapas* bars all over Spain and Portugal.

This pepper is typically sweet, but sometimes fiery (about 10 to 15%), which explains the popular Galician aphorism, "*Os pementos de Padrón, uns pican e outros non."* ("Padrón peppers, some are hot, some are not"). The only way to ascertain whether a Padrón pepper is hot or not is to eat it. For what it's worth, Bina and I can now claim to have eaten Padrón peppers in Padrón itself.

With all this touristing, our two days in Padrón passed pleasantly, although the second day off the trail turned out to be unnecessary. It clouded up on Wednesday but never rained, so we could have continued on our way that morning. No matter. We had enjoyed researching the St. James story in Padrón.

And for our troubles, the tourist office there had even issued us a document (in Latin) called the *Pedronía,* testifying that we had visited the major sites related to the Apostle. It bore the subtitle, *Hic Fuit Corpus Beati Jacobi,* or, "This was the body of St. James."

We had also enjoyed some good meals at the Hotel Chef Rivera, whose Señor Rivera had once cheffed at a deluxe restaurant elsewhere in Spain. Finally, and no small matter, we had taken full advantage of the coin-operated laundry across the street, a blessing after all the days of washing clothes in hotel sinks.

Now, we were well rested to begin the final stage of our saunter into Santiago de Compostela.

19

TO THE EMERALD CITY

The distance from Padrón to Santiago de Compostela is 24 km, well within the range of a one-day walk. Bina and I, however, had decided to make this a two-day trip by stopping for the night in O Milladoiro, a bedroom community of Santiago. This would leave us only six kilometers to cover on the second day, enabling us to reach the cathedral in time for the noon Pilgrim's Mass. This Mass, which is held every day to welcome arriving *peregrinos*, would provide the capstone to our Camino.

On the morning of September 6, the Hotel Chef Rivera came alive in the pre-dawn hours as *peregrinos* began stirring in their rooms, opening their doors and clumping down the wooden stairs to have breakfast. Since this racket started as early as 6 a.m., we assumed that most of this crowd was intending to walk all the way to Santiago.

Bina and I planned a more leisurely pace and didn't get out of bed until 7:30. By the time we sat down for breakfast, the only *peregrino* left in the hotel, other than ourselves, was a dark-haired young woman lingering over her pastry and coffee. When we encountered her later that day on the trail, we learned that she was a Greek from Cyprus.

Leaving the hotel at 9:15, we found a cloudy day with cool temperatures in the mid-60s. Our path out of town took us past the St. Mary's church in Iria Flavia and then a short distance along the N-550 highway, which goes directly to Santiago de Compostela. You could drive there in 40 minutes.

At the small town of Pazos, the Camino veered off from this busy road and we began walking down country lanes that link a succession of farming villages. The closer we got to Santiago, the more prosperous these communities appeared — plenty of new construction and refurbishment going on. We surmised that many of these properties belonged to people who commuted to good jobs in the city.

In the town of Rúa de Francos, we stopped in the local church to obtain a *sello*. As the priest took us into a room behind the sanctuary to retrieve his stamp pad, we noticed the walls covered with small, primitive paintings. Most seemed to be from the 19th or early 20th centuries and incorporated written testimonials from local parishioners thanking the saints or the Virgin Mary for helping them through some great trial in their life.

One painting, for example, portrayed a steam boat wallowing in high seas. The inscription below related how one Enrique Uzal Ródriguez, sailing for America, had encountered a tempest on the high seas and implored the Virgin to rescue him. Such popular piety is touching in a way that the grandest church altars are not.

Testimonies of faith.

In another small church a short distance away, we found a glass case containing an English translation of a two-page poem, or prayer, written by a Franciscan monk named Fray Dino La Faba. The verses explore the idea that simply walking the Camino is insufficient if you fail to search for God along the way:

Though I had seen all the monuments
and contemplated the best sunsets;
though I had learned a greeting in every language;
and drank the fresh water from all springs;
if I have not found who the maker
of such beauty and peace is,
I have arrived nowhere.

Shortly before arriving in O Milladoiro, we began noticing inscriptions of another kind: signs and banners, posted on private houses, protesting about waste removal (*limpa de residuos* in Galician) and a company called "Toysal." The locals, it seemed, were quite riled up about this Toysal. As I discovered later via Google, Toysal is a waste management company based in Vigo that had applied to build a treatment plant in an old quarry in the nearby town of Casalonga. The locals were objecting to the 40 truck loads of waste that would be delivered to the plant daily.

Couldn't blame them. But it's worth noting that protest signs are not uncommon in Spain. We rarely saw that in Portugal, where people seem content — at least right now — to go about their daily business. Within minutes after crossing the ferry into Spain, however, we started seeing wall graffiti that equated capitalism with terrorism.

The roots of some of this left/right tension goes back 80 years. Watching the news one morning in our hotel in Vigo, I noticed that the big story of the day was an effort by leftist legislators to exhume the body of former dictator Francisco Franco and transfer it from a state mausoleum to a private family cemetery. The ashes of the Spanish Civil War, which ended in 1939, are apparently still flickering.

Yet, the more threatening political tension in Spain today involves regional separatism, particularly in the north of the country, in Catalonia, Galicia and the Basque country. When Bina and I traveled to Barcelona, a few weeks after finishing the Camino, we found the city festooned with Catalonian flags and banners. The day before, a million people had marched in the streets for independence. The banners, hung from apartment balconies all over the city, demanded the return of "political prisoners." The reference was to Catalan politicians who had been arrested or fled the country in the wake of a failed independence referendum in October 2017.

Our landlady in Barcelona made no secret of her pro-separatist feelings, emphatically stating that she preferred to speak Catalan, avoiding Spanish whenever possible. Since we knew no Catalan, we could only converse with her in English.

We found some of that attitude in Galicia, which is very proud of Galego, its provincial language. Galego bears more linguistic similarity to Portuguese than to Spanish, although it utilizes a lot of Castilian vocabulary and spelling. Official signs in Galicia are in both languages. While wandering around Pontevedra's medieval festival, I had noticed how Galicians like to celebrate their Celtic-rooted folk culture with bagpipe music. Listening to the street musicians piping away you'd think you were in Scotland.

The question is whether there's more here than historical nostalgia. While we did see plenty of Galicia-for-the-Galicians graffiti as we walked north from Vigo, it's not as full-throated as in Catalonia. Lacking the powerful economic engine of Barcelona, Galicians seem more aware of their dependence on the rest of Spain. As a taxi driver we met in Santiago put it: "All of this independence talk — it's like a kid wanting to move out of the family house and demanding that his parents pay the rent."

On the outskirts of O Milladoiro, we caught up with with the Greek Cypriot woman we had seen that morning in the hotel. It was now nearing 4 p.m. and she planned to continue all the way into Santiago that evening, which involved at least another two hours of walking. We didn't envy her, since we were now fairly tired and happy to call it a day. Saying goodbye to her, we left the Camino path and headed in the direction of the Hotel Payro, which was located in one of O Milladoiro's major shopping areas.

On the way, we stopped at a restaurant to have a late lunch. While waiting for our food, an old man at an adjacent table ventured a conversation with us in Spanish. He had noticed the scallop shells hanging from our backpacks and wanted to register his opinion about them.

"In the old days," he said, "pilgrims earned the right to those shells *after* they reached the cathedral in Santiago. Nowadays, you wear them before you get there. I don't understand that."

From a historical perspective, the man was quite correct. Medieval pilgrims acquired their scallop shells after completing their pilgrimage, not before.[1] Bina, whose Spanish is better than mine, tried to explain that modern *peregrinos* essentially display the shells to identify themselves to other pilgrims. It's a way of saying, "Hey, I take this pilgrimage stuff seriously and here's the scallop shell to prove it."

I'm not sure if she got the message across, but the man nodded at her, somewhat placated. He probably just wanted to get something off his chest.

O Milladoiro turned out to be a happening kind of place, with modern, trendy shops, such as Patagonia, and an eclectic mix of restaurants to attract the younger crowd. There was an Irish Pub right across the street from our hotel. The Payro itself, a family-run establishment, offered clean, comfortable rooms, but no breakfast. When we expressed our concern to the owner about finding eggs in the morning — our constant battle in Spain — he kindly walked across the street to the Irish pub and asked them to prepare omelettes for us the next morning. This enabled us to begin our final walk into Santiago on a full stomach — which turned out to be a blessing, given the long day ahead of us.

We hoisted our packs for one last time at 8:45 a.m. on Friday, September 7, with the temperature starting in the low 70s. We expected to encounter mostly urban sprawl all the way to the Santiago cathedral. Instead, just outside of Milladoiro, we crossed some wooded, shady terrain, passing by a few farms and gardens. Soon we were ascending a range of hills that offered views of Santiago in the valley below.

I can best liken our feelings to those of Dorothy as she approached the Emerald City of Oz at the end of her long trek on the Yellow Brick Road. With my camera's long-range lens, I could just make out the cathedral towers poking up in the haze amid a cluster of more modern buildings. The goal of our long journey from Porto was now in sight — if we could just get the navigation right.

Like any large city, Santiago has a lot of streets leading into it. The two apps that we were running on our phones, *Wisely* and *Flannery,* didn't always agree on the best approach. Several times, we found ourselves following the roadside obelisks, or yellow arrows, only to suddenly notice that we had ventured off the "official" route. Initially, this proved rather frustrating, until it occurred to us that all roads into Santiago de Compostela ultimately lead to the cathedral. So, why worry?

We weren't the only ones confused in this way. Numerous groups of pilgrims were heading for the cathedral, most of them, no doubt, eager to attend the noon Mass. At one point, we found a large gaggle of them stopped at the intersection of two roads as they studied their apps or paper maps. One sign labelled "Conxo" pointed to the right, the other "Santa Marta," to the left. Studying *Wisely*, I could see that both roads led to the cathedral. The only difference appeared to be that Santa Marta crossed more major highways and appeared more direct. Conxo would take us down some side streets before rejoining the Santa Marta route close to the city center.

Most of the *peregrinos* at the intersection opted for Santa Marta — in fact, Wisely recommended doing that. Feeling a bit contrarian that morning, Bina and I decided to take the Conxo way, to avoid the crowds and the highway traffic. This route did, indeed, take us on a quiet stroll through the suburbs. We encountered only one other *peregrino* until we reached the Avenida de Juan Carlos I, where our route merged back into the Santa Marta. There, our relative solitude ended, as we joined the flow of fellow of pilgrims passing through the Alameda Park before entering Santiago's old city.

The transition is abrupt. There's no castle wall or drawbridge to cross. One moment you're walking through a modern urban area, then you cross a street and you're entering a more medieval-like environment. Or, at least, older. As you proceed down the winding narrow lanes to the cathedral, you actually glimpse a jumble of architectural styles, from Gothic to 19th century, as befits a city that's nearly 1,000 years old.

But what really confirms your sense of having "arrived" in Santiago de Compostela is all the tourists and pilgrims. The streets are choked with them — the tourists sauntering around with cameras, peering into shop windows or perusing cafe menus, the pilgrims with backpacks striding purposefully toward the cathedral, their faces beaming with anticipation.

Like us. We hurried through the old town, with scarcely a glance from side to side, looking ahead to that magical moment when we would turn the corner and find ourselves at the cathedral. When you first enter the old quarter, the buildings towering above you block out any sight of the cathedral towers, so you don't know you're there until you are.

Although I quickly checked the *Wisely* app once or twice, I needn't have bothered. All we had to do was follow the general flow of pilgrims down a lane known as the Rua do Franco until we turned a corner and finally saw the cathedral towers rising up at the other end.

------

1. See Appendix Two, "The Scallop Shell."

20

TREASURE THE MOMENT

There is a ritual that most modern pilgrims perform when they reach the cathedral. Rather than entering the church itself, they head for the Praza do Obradoiro.

This is the huge square facing the most scenic side of the cathedral, the monumental entrance known as the Pórtico de la Gloria. There, they finally get to release the pent-up emotions built up over the long journey. Some fall on their knees to cry or pray. Others rush around excitedly hugging each other and taking photos. A few had just set their backpacks down and were stretched out on the pavement basking in the sun, smiling dreamily.

Bina and I said nothing as we walked into the Praza and turned to stare at the cathedral looming up before us. This is a moment for feeling, not thinking. We just turned to each other for a long embrace, letting the feelings of gratitude, joy, relief and accomplishment pour out of us. Bina sobbed into my shoulder as all those emotions overtook her, and I felt myself choking up as well. After a few minutes, we held hands and thanked God for guiding our steps and helping us complete our Camino.

Celebrating the moment.

Once we had regained our composure, we asked another *peregrino* to take the obligatory photo of us standing before the cathedral, which provides a magnificent backdrop for the completion of the Camino. The largest Romanesque church in Spain, with later Baroque additions, the cathedral is at its most impressive when viewed from the Praza. From no other angle can you appreciate the soaring majesty of the Romanesque facade and the wedding cake intricacy of the Baroque towers.

It was now after 11 a.m. and we paused from our wonderment to discuss our plans for the afternoon. We still needed to attend the Pilgrim's Mass at noon, get our Compostelas from the Pigrims Office, check into our hotel and find lunch. Entering the cathedral and finding a seat for Mass required ditching our backpacks, since church security allows people to enter only with purses and small handbags. We knew there was an office somewhere on the opposite side of the church that stored backpacks. But finding it took a good 20 minutes, since the cathedral is surrounded by a multitude of small shops.

Once inside the church, we found every pew full, which was a bit of a surprise since we entered at 11:30, half an hour early. Bina sat on the stone floor next to a pillar catty corner to the altar while I stood behind her. The first time the congregation rose during the service, she found that she needed my help getting up, as her legs had gone stiff sitting on the cold stone floor.

What makes this service a Pilgrims Mass is that the it begins with an announcement of the number of pilgrims who have received their Compostelas during the last 24 hours, where they came from and where they started their pilgrimage. The priest then bestows a special blessing on all these *peregrinos,* who represent an extensive array of nationalities.

We were hoping that this service would include the famous *botafumeiro*, a massive incense burner that swings from the cathedral ceiling. But operating the *botafumeiro* (Galician for "smoke expeller") requires eight trained men, known as *tiraboleiros,* to pull on the ropes to operate the pulleys. The church only performs this ritual if some group agrees to pay 450 euros for the performance — typically a tour company that wants to reward its clients. That was, unfortunately, not to be the case for this Mass, so we would have to wait for another opportunity.

As soon as the Mass ended at 1 p.m., we went to find the Pilgrims Office, located a couple of blocks away, to get our *Compostelas,* or "get-out-of-hell-free card," as some style it. We had dreaded performing this errand, having read about the long lines usually involved. And we did have to queue up for about an hour before we reached the counter lined with volunteers, who scrutinize each person's *sellos*, or stamps. The woman I dealt with gave mine only a cursory glance and then printed out my certificate, in Latin, and handed it to me.

I received the Latin version because of the way I had answered the question: what was your motivation in walking the Camino? The Church provides three possible answers: religious, spiritual or cultural. I had picked "spiritual," which is sort of a combination of religious and cultural.

In addition to our Compostelas, which are provided free, Bina and I both paid a small additional fee, 3 euros, for distance certificates, also in Latin. These documents certify where you began your pilgrimage and how many kilometers you walked. Ours credit us for 280 km from Porto to Santiago de Compostela, the official distance, although we walked 317 km (197 miles) by our own calculations.

The attendants in the Pilgrims Office move expeditiously, no doubt to keep that long line moving, and we were out of there in less than five minutes. An English man standing next to me at the counter was not so lucky. He had ridden to Santiago on his bicycle but had failed to understand that two *sellos*, rather than just one, were required for each day of the last 200 kilometers (100 km for walkers). He was still arguing with the volunteer when I left the counter.

Bina and I made our way back to the Praza do Obradoiro to take some photos to record our achievement, displaying our *Compostelas* and distance certificates proudly. While chatting with some other *peregrinos* in the Praza, we learned that there was a strong likelihood that the *botafumerio* would be swung at Mass that evening.

So, after checking in at our hotel and having a belated lunch, we returned to the cathedral at 6 p.m, a full one and a half hours before the 7:30 p.m. Mass. Our pilgrimage wouldn't be complete without seeing the *botafumeiro* and we were determined to arrive early enough to get good seats.

We plopped ourselves down in an empty pew in the transept

to the side of the altar. The first two or three rows of pews were roped off as *reservada* (reserved), likely for the tour group that would be paying for the *botafumeiro* display that evening. Studying the arrangement of the pulley mechanism on the ceiling, I figured that if the *botafumeiro* did swing this evening, its arc would carry the incense burner right over our heads. So, there we sat for the next hour and a half, taking turns to walk around and admire the massive cathedral interior.

This provided us the opportunity to visit the crypt of St. James himself, which is located underneath the altar. You get there by strolling along the ambulatory, a semi-circular walkway behind the altar, until you find an entrance with a green light above it. There I stood in line for about 15 minutes as the attendant waved us in by groups of five or so.

When my turn came, I descended a narrow staircase into a small subterranean chapel with a white marble altar. A recess in the wall behind the altar held a silver casket that supposedly contained the bones of St. James. The medieval accounts reporting the discovery of these relics are contradictory and the church itself didn't render an official verdict until 1884, when Pope Leo XIII visited the crypt and declared the remains to be those of the Apostle.

By the time 7:30 rolled around, the cathedral was back to standing room only for late arriving attendees. Bina and I were glad we had claimed our seats early. We were also feeling encouraged that we might actually see the *botafumeiro* this time, since a tour group now occupied the *reservada* section.

Burning incense during a Mass is a common Catholic ritual designed to symbolize the prayers of the faithful rising to heaven. As Psalm 141:2 says: "Let my prayer be directed as incense in thy sight: the lifting up of my hands, as evening sacrifice." But why all the excitement about this particular church fumigation? How had it become such a tourist draw?

The Santiago *botafumeiro* is the largest in Spain and one of the largest in the world. Crafted in 1851 of a brass and bronze alloy and plated in silver, this censer (also known as a thurible) weighs 117 pounds and measures five feet tall. For many pilgrims, watching the *botafumeiro* swing has simply become an essential part of finishing the Camino. You can't go home without it.

As soon as the priests had finished communion and removed the liturgical cups and plates, the brown-robed *botafumeiro* crew stepped forward to grab the ropes. Half the congregation immediately rose to their feet, cell phones at the ready. The church does not permit the use of cameras during Mass, a rule enforced by watchful attendants. But nobody is going to confiscate hundreds of phone cameras.

Bina and I began clicking away with the rest of them as the censer began its stately swing across the transept in an ever-widening rhythmic arc. At full speed, it resembled an enormous flying dragon, breathing smoke over our heads.

Can't miss this.

So there, we had seen it, a final check on our list of Things-to-

Do in Santiago de Compostela. But what, at the end of the day, had the Camino experience actually meant to us? I'll let Bina speak for herself on that matter:

"One of the reasons I wanted to walk the *Senda Litoral* is because I have always felt God's presence strongest by the ocean. While praying as we walked along the coast, I felt a buoyancy and lightness of spirit that comes from being in the presence of God, surrounded by God's amazing creation."

For me, less certainty. If God whispered in my ear somewhere along the trail, I wasn't listening properly at the time. On the other hand, I did engage in plenty of self-examination. When you spend long hours walking, you can't help but think about past events and ruminate over what you would have done differently had you known better. I can't say that I was struck by any great revelations, though. By the time a person reaches his mid-60s, personal faults are unlikely to come as any great surprise.

During the actual process of walking the Camino, I had often found myself focused on logistical issues — getting from point A to point B, finding places to eat, planning the next day's walk, etc. A more spiritual understanding of the Camino experience had to wait until we had arrived in Santiago and had more time for reflection.

For me, that process began one morning when we attended an English language Mass in one of the side chapels in the cathedral, known as the Chapel of Our Lady of Soledad.

Bina and I found this service more meaningful than the official Pilgrims Mass a few days before. We understood it, for one thing — the cathedral's major services are conducted in Spanish — and we enjoyed singing the music in English translation. That enables you to give voice to your feelings. We were also delighted to receive a personal blessing from the Filipino priest who officiated.

As Lutheran Protestants, Bina and I cannot accept the wine and bread during a Catholic Communion. In the U.S., however, whenever we attended a Catholic Mass, we were accustomed to approaching the priest during communion with our arms crossed to receive a blessing. Our attempt to do that at the Pilgrims Mass had been met by a baffled stare from the Spanish priest. Apparently this doesn't happen much in Spain, which is mostly a Catholic country. A security guard, who was standing nearby, had to lean over and whisper instructions to the priest on how to handle us.

By contrast, the Filipino priest officiating at the English Mass understood precisely what to do, which certainly provided a more comfortable experience for Bina and myself. Father Manny Domingo went even further by taking the time to bestow a longish blessing upon us, giving thanks for our presence in the church that day, for our being able to finish our Camino, for our families who enabled us to undertake this pilgrimage and for God to protect us during our subsequent journeys in life. It was actually the nicest, sweetest blessing we had ever received from a Catholic priest.

At the end of the Mass, an Irish woman named Colette mentioned that the Pilgrims Office would host a "Camino reflection group" at 2 that afternoon. When we arrived at the second floor office, we were greeted by Father Noel Brady, from Melbourne, Australia, and Sister Mary, an Irish nun. Sister Mary mostly deferred to Father Brady to run the meeting.

Now in his mid-70s and retired from full-time priestly work, Brady had hiked several different Camino routes, as well as other pilgrimage trails in France and Italy. He knew how to relate to fellow *peregrinos* and put them at their ease.

"Call me 'Pere Noel,' or 'Father Christmas'," he said brightly, when waving us into our chairs. "Noel" is the French word for "Christmas."

We were joined by Rufus and Dawn, a younger couple from Scotland. The four of us agreed that the Camino experience had impressed us deeply, particularly the joy we all found in reducing the clutter in our lives. Walking the Camino is a good way to get back to the basics of life — food, shelter and companionship — without all the complexities of our day-to-day existence back home. For a time, at least, you don't have to worry about taking your car into the shop or how to fund your retirement.

Picking up on that thread, Father Noel contributed an insight that he had obtained on his walks, which is the importance of living in the moment and not taking anything in life for granted. "You should live as if you're going to die tonight," he said. "Why? Because yesterday is just a memory and tomorrow a vision."

If only today matters, Father Noel continued, warming to his theme, it then becomes very important how you treat others today. "Look at the behavior of people when their airplane is about to crash, or when they face some similar disaster. Their first instinct is not to stuff themselves with the luxuries of life. Instead, they grab a cell phone to try and call or text the people who matter the most to them and tell them they love them. At the end, that's what matters."

Ironically, as we were returning to our hotel afterward, I saw a man cross the street wearing a T-shirt with this message on the back: "The important things in life are not things."

There seemed to be a theme here. Thinking back over my Camino experience, I treasure the memory of the weeks that Bina and I spent on the trail because the experience helped bring us closer together as a couple. Even though we had been married for 30 years, we had spent much of that time focused on our parental duties or individual careers.

Walking the Camino provided us a welcome opportunity to spend time with each other without other pressing claims on our attention. As you focus on the really important relationships in your life, you begin to realize that so much else going on around you day to day is just background noise.

Bina and I had also strengthened our personal bond through a sense of shared achievement. When we stood together in front of the cathedral, we had celebrated a joint accomplishment. We had researched and planned the trip together over many long months. We had then walked together, all the way from Porto to Santiago de Compostela, as a couple. We had overcome the numerous challenges along the way, as a team. No me or her, just us. This represented an accomplishment for us to relish — as a couple.

At the recommendation of Father Noel, Bina and I later visited the Pilgrims Museum, which is located across the street from the cathedral. We spent an hour perusing the exhibits, which detail the history of the Camino de Santiago and religious pilgrimages in general. One display that caught my eye high-lighted some verses by the Spanish poet Antonio Machado (1875-1939):

> Wanderer, your footsteps are the road,
> and nothing more; wanderer, there is
> no road, the road is made by walking.
> By walking, one makes the road,
> and upon glancing behind one sees
> the path that never will be trod again.
> Wanderer, there is no road —
> Only wakes upon the sea.

It came to me then that this might be the best lesson I could take from the Camino de Santiago: live in the present and treasure the moment.

APPENDIX ONE: ST. JAMES

During his ministry, Jesus attracted 12 principal disciples, or Apostles. "Apostle" is ancient Greek for "the one who was sent away/off on a mission." This term was attached to those men for their role in assisting Jesus during his ministry and then spreading Christianity around the Mediterranean world following the crucifixion.

The Gospels list two Jameses among the twelve. To distinguish them, later church writers labelled one as "James the Greater," and the other, "James the Lesser." The biographical details on this second James are a bit fuzzy. He may or may not have been the brother or kinsman of Jesus. In any case, James the Greater is the one linked to the Camino de Santiago.

The Bible tells us a fair amount about this James, who came from Bethsaida, near the Sea of Galilee. He was the son of Zebedee, a fisherman, and Mary Salomé. James and his brother John, who was later credited with authoring the Gospel of John, became the first followers of Jesus.

Mark 1:19-20 relates how Jesus "saw James son of Zebedee and his brother John, who were in their boat mending the nets.

Immediately he called them; and they left their father Zebedee in the boat with the hired men, and followed him."

Note the reference to "hired men." This suggests the father was a step above the common run of fishermen, since he could afford to crew his boat. So, while James and John can still be classified as humble fishermen, they likely enjoyed some standing in their community. Zebedee steps out of the story at this point. But Salome, James' mother, followed Jesus as well and is mentioned by Mark as present at the crucifixion and the subsequent opening of Christ's empty tomb.

Jesus seems to have had a special fondness for the two brothers, particularly John, who is described several times in the Gospels as "the beloved disciple." Both of them, along with Peter, were privileged to witness Jesus' Transfiguration. As the four of them climbed a mountain to pray, Jesus became outlined by bright rays of light and a voice from the sky called him "Son," as in, "this is my Son, the Beloved; with him I am well pleased; listen to him!" (Matthew 17:5)

Jesus nicknamed the brothers the "Sons of Thunder," suggesting that they may have had a temper. Luke 9:51-56 relates how the brothers asked Jesus to rain fire down upon a Samaritan village that declined to receive him on his way to Jerusalem. "But he turned and rebuked them."

Mark 10:35-45 tells of another rebuke to the brothers when they asked Jesus if they would be privileged to sit with him in heaven, "one at your right hand and one at your left, in your glory." Jesus responded that such a favor "is not mine to grant" but rather is reserved for the Father. In Matthew 20:20-28, however, the offending request actually comes from Mary Salome, the mother of the two brothers.

Apparently jealous of all the attention the brothers were receiving from Jesus, the other ten disciples "began to get angry with James and John," according to Mark. This prompted Jesus to lecture them as well: "You know that among the Gentiles those whom they recognize as their rulers lord it over them ... but whoever wishes to become great among you must be the slave of all."

The last mention of James in the Bible involves his martyrdom following Jesus' death. As related in Acts 12:1-2, "About that time King Herod laid violent hands upon some who belonged to the church. He had James, the brother of John, killed with the sword." Some scholars have questioned this Biblical wording because a swift form of execution, such as decapitation by the sword, was typically reserved for Roman citizens, a status that famously applied to St. Paul but not to the Apostle James. It is possible, however, that James died by the sword in a crueler, more drawn-out process.

Other Apostles became martyrs as well, according to later church tradition. The fact that James' martyrdom is the only one specifically cited in the Bible suggests that he was the first to suffer this fate.

At that point, the written record on James goes silent for more than 800 years. Then, we begin to find in church documents mentions of legends, or traditions that move the locus of the James story from Palestine all the way to the Iberian Peninsula. These likely derived from oral stories relating to James that were passed around in the centuries following Christ's death and finally written down in the ninth century.

There are two threads to this tradition. One relates that James traveled to Spain before his martyrdom to evangelize in what were then the prosperous Roman provinces of Galicia and Zaragoza. The second story returns his body Spain following his execution by King Herod. It seems that a boat guided by angels carried the Apostle's remains to the Roman port of Iria Flavia (near modern Padrón). His followers then buried him further inland at Mount Libredón.

Sometime in the 820s, a shepherd tending his flock in the area followed a play of lights in the sky to an ancient burial site on the mountain. He reported his discovery to the local bishop, who attributed the remains to St. James. A church was then built on the site, around which grew the city of Santiago de Compostela. How did the city get that name?

"Santiago" is the easy part. It's the Spanish for "James," derived originally from the Hebrew form of James, "Ya'akov." Starting with "Santo" (Saint) "Yago" (James), the Spanish evolves, over time, into "Santiago." But what about "Compostela?"

The commonly accepted assumption is that this name combines two Latin words: "campus" (field) and "stellae" (of the stars). That gives us "St. James of the field of stars," a mellifluous phrasing that dovetails nicely with the shepherd discovery story.

However, it's also possible that "Compostela" actually comes from two other Latin words: "compositum" (arranged or well-ordered) and "tellus" (field). As Roman Latin evolved into popular or Vulgar Latin during the Middle Ages, the two words put together came to designate a burial ground, or cemetery, essentially a field where things are arranged. By this interpretation, Santiago de Compostela simply means "Burial Place of St. James," not nearly as romantic.

By the 12th century, this burial site in Santiago de Compostela was attracting pilgrims from all over Europe. The various routes of this pilgrimage became known as the "Way of St. James," or, in Spanish, the "Camino de Santiago."

APPENDIX TWO: THE SCALLOP SHELL

When Bina and I first began planning our Camino walk toward the end of 2017, she went online to order a product that she said we must carry on our backpacks all the way to Santiago de Compostela.

At $6.95 each, these turned out to be white scallop shells with the cross of St. James painted red on the side curving outward and a red cord looped through a hole in the top. We used the cord to hang the shells from our packs as we walked the 200 miles from Porto, Portugal, to Santiago de Compostela in Spain — same as most of the other *peregrinos* (pilgrims) we encountered.

Utilizing the scallop shell in this manner derives from a very old tradition. As stated in the *Liber Sancti Iacobi* (Book of St. James), a 12th century guide for *peregrinos*, "It is not without reason that the pilgrims returning from the threshold of St. James bear shells."

Medieval pilgrims would generally undertake their journey at the instruction of their local priest as penance for their sins. When they returned home, they needed some way of proving that they had actually walked the full route — a souvenir of the journey, if you will.

For those walking the Camino de Santiago, the scallop shell evolved as the souvenir of choice. It already carried a lot of religious symbolism. Since pre-Christian times, depictions of scallop shells had been used in funeral imagery to communicate the concept of an afterlife. The early Church appropriated this symbolism, which became particularly common in Spain during the Visgothic period (6th to 8th centuries). The Visgothic depiction of the scallop shell, however, featured the concave, or inward-curving, side. The later St. James version emphasizes the convex, or rounded side.

The Church also used the shell as a symbol of baptism, or rebirth. Baptismal fonts in medieval churches often carry representations of scallop shells. At some point, this symbolism became attached to the story of St. James.

A popular legend associated with the Apostle involves a knight riding his horse on the Atlantic cliffs as the boat carrying James' body from Palestine approached the coast. The animal bolted upon seeing the boat and plummeted into the sea with its rider. St. James, or his spirit, miraculously intervened and saved the knight, who emerged from the water covered in scallop shells.

It also helped that the scallop shell is easily found on the beaches of the Galician coast, just to the west of Santiago de Compostela. Pilgrims who visited the Santiago cathedral could continue on to the town of Finisterre, on the coast, to collect their shell right off the beach. During their homeward journey, they would typically wear the shell on their hats or some other item of clothing, such as the *scarcella*, or purse.

Over time, entrepreneurs recognized a business opportunity in removing that inconvenient trip. By the middle of the 12th century, according to the *Liber Sancti Iacobi*, pilgrims could purchase scallop shells at the door to the cathedral itself. The industry grew to the point that vendors were licensed.

Considered from that perspective, people who sell scallop

shells today are also carrying on a long-established Camino tradition. The major difference from medieval times is that today's pilgrims wear the shell on their journey toward Santiago, rather than on the way back. After all, most board a bus, train or plane after completing the pilgrimage rather than actually *walk* home.

APPENDIX THREE: TIPS FOR WALKING THE CAMINO

There are few absolute rules when walking the Camino de Santiago because individual circumstances and capabilities vary greatly. What works for one person in terms of strategy, planning and equipment may prove unsatisfactory for another. With that caveat, Bina and I did learn some lessons walking the *Caminho Portugues* that we would like to pass on to readers who might be considering doing the pilgrimage for the first time:

1. Pick your Camino carefully. There are at least seven major pilgrimage routes to Santiago de Compostela and they vary greatly in terms of length and difficulty of terrain. You need to determine the path that best suits your age, level of physical conditioning and overall health. Bina and I selected the coastal variation of the *Caminho Portugues* because it featured mostly flat terrain and sufficient infrastructure, such as lodging, restaurants and cafes.
2. One useful tool for analyzing the various Camino routes is the Spanish language Website gronze.com,

which shows terrain elevations, as well as distances between stages and available lodging.

3. A good GPS-based smartphone app to use when actually walking the Camino is *Wisely Pilgrim*. With *Wisely*, it's virtually impossible to get lost on the trail, since your progress is always displayed on the map. *Wisely* also shows distances between towns and most of the lodging and food facilities you encounter along the way.

4. Our go-to Website for researching the nitty gritty details of walking the Camino was the Camino de Santiago Forum hosted by Ivar Rekve. For virtually any Camino-related subject you can think of, you're almost certain to find a discussion on Rekve's forum. Revke also maintains a luggage depository in Santiago de Compostela to which *peregrinos* can ship excess gear for safekeeping until they arrive.

5. On Facebook, check out groups such as *American Pilgrims on the Camino*, as well as individual groups for each Camino route. *Caminho Portuguese Pilgrims*, for example, proved particularly helpful to us.

6. To reserve lodging, we utilized booking.com, which contains useful ratings and reviews of the properties it offers. We often double-checked those reviews with TripAdvisor. As a general rule, pick those places that offer free cancellation in case you have to adjust your schedule.

7. Uber is another useful app. Service is not available everywhere and is particularly scarce in rural parts of Spain and Portugal. But given the difficulties of calling taxis in a foreign country, Uber can save you a lot of aggravation and waiting time if a driver is available.

8. Footwear is very much an individual issue, since everyone's feet are different. Any good outfitter store

will carry a bewildering array of brands and styles. For what it's worth, I went with a hiking shoe (Keen Targhee III) and Bina a trail runner (Hoka One One Stinson ATR 4). Both proved satisfactory on the terrain we encountered on the Portuguese Coastal.

9. Nothing can hobble a Camino faster than blisters. Our strategy to avoid same was to wear Darn Tough merino wool socks with Injinji liners. We also lubricated our feet each morning — me with Hike Goo and Bina with Footglide. This combination of lubrication, socks and liners kept us blister-free during the entire walk.

10. For daypacks, I carried a Gregory Zulu 30 and Bina an Osprey Tempest 20. No complaints with either, although people who carry all their equipment on their backs each day will need larger packs. Bina and I actually packed most of our clothing and gear in two roller bags and then hired a luggage transfer service to move it from lodging to lodging.

11. Tuitrans, a Spanish-based company that operates on the Camino routes between Porto and Santiago de Compostela, won our business for luggage transfer. We found them to be efficient and responsive in getting our roller bags from place to place.

12. When it comes to clothes — pants, shirts and underwear — go for synthetic, quick-dry fabrics whenever possible. This kind of specialized clothing will cost you more. But the expense is well worth it when you can dry your clothes overnight after a wash in the sink. You do not want to carry damp clothes to your next destination.

13. Don't overpack. This is the classic mistake of all newbie *peregrinos.* If you've never before done a long walk like this, your imagination can run wild thinking

of all the things you *might* need on a long walk. As Bina likes to say, "You pack your fears." But you're really better off confining yourself to the must-haves, rather than the like-to-haves.

14. Be diligent about collecting *sellos*, or stamps, for your *Credencial del Peregrino*. To receive your *Compostela*, or certificate of completion, from the Pilgrims Office in Santiago de Compostela, you must prove that you walked the last 100 km of the journey (or cycled the last 200 km). You do that by showing two stamps collected for each day of that final stretch. You might get away with missing a *sello* or two, but the last 100/200 km requirement is non-negotiable. It does you no good to walk for hundreds of kilometers early in your trip and then bus or train the last 100 km to Santiago. You will not be granted a *Compostela*.

APPENDIX FOUR: LODGING ALONG THE PORTUGUESE CAMINO (COASTAL VARIATION)

Our journey from Porto to Santiago de Compostela took us 17 walking days, not including rest days. Details of each of those days, with photos, can be found at *Two Clines Traveling*, a blog compiled by my wife, Bina.

The following is a list of those 17 stages, with kilometers walked and comments on lodging. We are, by no means, claiming that these are the best lodging choices available in each locality. We are simply saying that these represented the best compromise between value and price that we found available on booking.com at the time we made the reservations.

1. Porto to Matosinhos. 12.8 km. **Porto apartment.**
   Excellent choice for long-term stay in Porto, with great access to the coastal Camino. Paula, the landlady, is very helpful and responsive.
2. Matosinhos to Vila Chã. 16 km. Porto apartment.
3. Vila Chã to Póvoa de Varzim. 19 km. Porto apartment.
4. Póvoa de Varzim to Esposende. 19 km. Porto apartment.
5. Esposende to Viana do Castelo. 19 km. **Dias House.**

Comfortable B&B with robust home-cooked breakfast to get you started in the morning. Only disadvantage is that it is located outside Viana do Castelo, so you can't explore that interesting city in the evening unless you taxi or Uber in.

6. Viana do Castelo do Castelo to Praia de Âncora. 22 km. **Albergaria Quim Barreiros.** Comfortable, modern hotel. Good location on waterfront.

7. Praia de Âncora to A Guarda. 20.6 km. **Hotel Celta.** An older property, but well maintained, in the center of town.

8. A Guarda to Villadesuso. 19 km. **Hotel Costa Verde.** Modern hotel with good restaurant on site.

9. Villadesuso to Baiona. 17.6 km. **Parador de Baiona** and **Hotel Rompeolas.** Parador is a luxury property, in a great location overlooking the marina with quick access to the center of town. We found it overpriced for the value received, however. Rompeolas is a better value for the money, right on the Camino, and offers a nice view overlooking the bay.

10. Baiona to Nigrán. 9.3 km. **El Retiro Hotel.** The hotel rooms are basic, but the restaurant is popular with locals. A few blocks from Camino.

11. Nigrán to Vigo. 20.3 km. **Hotel Oca Ipanema.** Comfortable, modern hotel in an area with lots of upscale restaurants and shopping. A 15-minute walk from the Camino.

12. Vigo to Arcade. 22 km. **Hotel Restaurante Isape.** Hotel and restaurant both good, with easy access to Camino.

13. Arcade to Pontevedra. 13.4 km. **Peregrino** and **Hotel Restaurante Rúas.** Peregrino is located right on the Camino at entrance to town. Features clean rooms and good cafe next door. Rúas is a much older hotel located in the center of the old city with good

restaurant on site. Quaint but noisy. Good access to Camino leaving Pontevedra.

14. Pontevedra to Caldas de Reis. 24.3 km. Hotel Rúas.

15. Caldas de Reis to Padrón. 20.9 km. **Hotel Chef Rivera.** Excellent restaurant on site and comfortable rooms. Good location near center of town just a few blocks from Camino. Also features a coin laundromat right across the street.

16. Padrón to O Milladoiro. 21.5 km. **Hotel Payro.** Nice family-run hotel with clean, modern rooms. A few blocks off Camino.

17. O Milladoiro to Santiago de Compostela. 9.5 km. **Nest Style Santiago.** Boutique hotel near entrance to old town. Good breakfasts at on-site restaurant. Rooms simple but reasonably comfortable.

ACKNOWLEDGMENTS

This book is a joint project of Kenneth and Bina Cline. The two of us planned our Camino de Santiago adventure together, walked the 200 miles together, and compiled the material for this account together.

While I wrote the basic narrative, based on notes taken at the time, Bina supplemented the story with her own recollections. She also contributed all the photos, many of which previously appeared in her blog of our walk, entitled Two Traveling Clines, published shortly after we we reached Santiago de Compostela. Finally, Bina copy edited the entire work. Without her assistance, this book would not have been possible.

I would also like to thank the El Cajon Writers Salon in Grecia, Costa Rica. This group of literary enthusiasts, which meets once a month in the home of Jim and Irina Just, provided invaluable feedback on early chapters. Group member Paul Hastings contributed some particularly helpful suggestions.

Finally, a special callout to George D. Greenia, Professor Emeritus of Hispanic Studies at the College of William & Mary — of which I am an alumnus (class of '76). One of the world's foremost experts on medieval pilgrimages, Greenia kindly agreed to review the historical details of my story of St. James (see Appendix One). He suggested several improvements that I gratefully incorporated into my account.

Of course, any remaining typos and inaccuracies of fact or interpretation are entirely my own.

ABOUT THE AUTHOR

Kenneth Cline is a former journalist who retired in July 2016 with thirty years of experience in newspaper and magazine writing, much of that devoted to financial services, history and travel. Most recently, he was managing editor of *BAI Banking Strategies* magazine.

He and his wife, Bina, currently live as "senior nomads." This means that they do not maintain a fixed abode, as such, but reside in different parts of the world at different times of the year.

The current work is the third in a series of travel books by Cline. The first, *Tracking the Queen of Sheba: A Travel Memoir of Yemen* (Amazon, 2016), related his adventures accompanying an archaeological expedition to the wilds of eastern Yemen in 1984. The second, *Village on the Nile: A Travel Memoir of Upper Egypt* (Amazon, 2017), described his experiences living in a village in Upper Egypt in 1983.

ALSO BY KENNETH CLINE

Tracking the Queen of Sheba: A Travel Memoir of Yemen

Village on the Nile: A Travel Memoir of Upper Egypt